BREATHE DEEP OR DIE SHALLOW

Tipping Life in Your Favor

Phillip W. Bufford

Copyright © 2008 by Phillip W. Bufford
Tip The Scale Consulting, LLC
www.tippingthescale.com

All rights reserved. No part of this book may be reproduced or transimitted in any form or by any means without written permission of the author. Published in the United States of America.

Edited by Chester Starks, Jr.
Photography by McKinley Wiley
Cover design by Pen To Press

ISBN: 978-0-9773496-1-6

Dedication

I dedicate this work to my dear parents, Rev. Eric & Debra Bufford.

Through everything Deana, Ericka and I put you through as kids, you remained available to us for direction and guidance. Pops, you're our hero. In a world where fathers are absent and irresponsible, you always clocked in on time, before time, and worked overtime as a faithful parent just to ensure we would be something more than a statistic. Thank you. Mom, thank you for allowing us the opportunity to express our feelings and thoughts without judgment or criticism. It wasn't an easy task but you did it nonetheless. You're our jewel and nothing before your time, in your time or after your time can ever compare. It's my hope I can empower others to Breathe Deep as both of you have empowered your children to do the same. So on behalf of my sisters and myself, we love you, thank you, and dedicate this work to you.

Now it's your turn to BREATHE DEEP as you enjoy the second part of your lives together – lives without your children living at home.

Well done Mom & Dad. Well Done!!!

Breathe Deep or Die Shallow

Table of Contents

Introduction	iii.
Preface	v.
Chapter 1: Give Me My Life Back	1
Building Your Platform	
• Foundations	2
• Remembering Your Dreams	12
• Assessing My Inventory	19
• Breaking Ground	33
Chapter 2: Thanks… but, No Thanks!	40
Discriminating Help	
• Drawing Lines in the Sand	41
• So You Say	55
• Yes You & No You	61
Chapter 3: Here We Go Again	68
Coping Frustrating Conversations	
• Who Am I Talking To	69
• Navigating Intimate Conflict	75
• Dead Weight Intimacy (DWI)	85
Chapter 4: I Need More Than This	95
Church is NOT Enough	
• Outgrowing Home	98
• Bible Spitters	106
• Damned To Hell	113
• Maintaining A Fresh Perspective	116
Chapter 5: YES FINALLY!	121
Tasting Small Success	
• Throw a Party	122
• The Judging Eye	125
• Keep It Moving	127

Table of Contents (continued)

Chapter 6: NO!!! This Can't Be Happening *Setbacks*	132
• Losing Perspective	134
• Remembering Your Platform	145
• Team Effort	156
Chapter 7: Haven't Seen You in a Minute *Fire from Past Flames*	161
• The Context	163
• The Encounter	165
• The Phone Calls	168
• The Visits	175
• The Reality	188
Chapter 8: This is My Story *Chronicling Your Journey*	198
• My Blood, Sweat, Tears	
Breathe Deep Reprise	203
About The Author	218
Acknowledgements	219

Introduction

All of us have experienced joy and sadness, excitement and fear. And while there are plenty of reactions we have to such experiences, one thing quite frequently happens when we're about to hear really bad or really good news– we take that infamous, self-bracing deep breath. That single deep breath braces us for what's coming next. That one deep breath becomes the bridge between reality and our worst fears or reality and dreams come true. When we discover a love one or a friend's life has come to a tragic end– we take that deep breath. When we're proposed to – we take that deep breath. When we hit the lottery – we take that deep breath. That single deep breath captures the magnitude of the moment. It demonstrates just how significant the experience truly is. And out of all of our breathing, that single deep breath is something we do on purpose!

This book is that single deep breath multiplied page by page. No longer will we live life on autopilot existing just because we exist. We're tired of shallow experiences, shallow relationships, shallow careers, and shallow memories. We know there's more to life than what we have and no longer are we waiting on someone to do for us what we should be doing for ourselves. We know what it feels like to be smothered by shallow people and dictated by shallow perspectives. Today, we refuse to slowly die to a shallow existence. Today, we tip the scale of life in our favor and we live on purpose. Today, we empower ourselves to create new behaviors, born from fresh perspectives, propelling us into a life of limitless possibilities!

Today, we breathe and we BREATHE DEEP!

Preface

In a world whereby life is shoved down our throats at a faster pace than we can fathom, it becomes very easy for us to lose ourselves in the demands of the day. Whether it is children, marital responsibilities, career demands, or simply attempting to arrange our personal lives into some semblance of order, we seem to undoubtedly be at the mercy of a life ongoing without end. We wrestle with aiming to accomplish tasks within 24 hours and become frustrated, saddened and even angered by the failure of our most valiant effort.

We seek to remedy our dilemmas by consolidating problems. We act as if intimate relationships can be treated like business transactions. We negotiate terms. We establish rules of reciprocity. We evaluate the pros and cons of such an endeavor. We make a commitment, not for its emotional significance but for its personal profit. And after the deal is done, we wonder why our relationships still fail. Our business day spills into our personal days. We speak to our kids like we talk to our staff. We argue with spouses like we fight with colleagues. We cannot tell when we are working or resting. And when we are sleeping, our minds are steadily preoccupied with situations for the following day, week, or month. We feel helpless to change the conditions of our lives. We run races we did not sign for. We fight battles we did not choose. We march to someone else's drum. We dance to someone else's rhythm. We live a life that is not our own and everything within us is screaming, "***GIVE ME MY LIFE BACK!!!!!***"

The truth to the matter is we have become slaves. We are slaves to a master with consciousness. It has much compassion. It cares very much about family. It has strong values. It does consider gender and it regards class highly. However, the catch is this slave master does all of this according to ITS OWN AGENDA. It drives us as it pleases. It pushes us as it feels. It puppets us on strings as it deems. It controls our lives. Though it could be an ally, we lack recognizing its significance and utilizing its potency. Therefore, we are forever sentenced to a cycle of SHALLOW and MEANINGLESS existence without any opportunity to control what we want to do with our lives because we cannot find anything in our lives satisfying to control. The culprit for these crimes is not the devil. The villain for these offences is not some outside force.

OUR VERY OWN PERSPECTIVES have incarcerated us! Our very own perceptions deny us what we so desperately desire. Our perspectives govern our comings and goings. It dictates what opportunities we will take and what opportunities we allow to pass. Through our perspectives, we view and carry out our own lives. It manages how we think and feel. And sadly is the case for many that you and I know, there are those who feel time have passed them by. Because of their perspective, they are convinced there is nothing they can do to salvage their life and so the action follows – they do nothing with their life. Simultaneously, there are others who allow their perspectives to drive and drain them until they have nothing left to offer. They are so driven by their perspectives of life and time they cannot even take time to breathe.

For these reasons, I have written this book. I write to you out of my own experiences, the experiences of others, counseling sessions, conversations, and referencing various authors. This book is not the END ALL BE ALL answer to the challenges facing us by our perceptions of life and time. It is only a response to the questions those challenges present. The topics of which I will take time to discuss here are topics another may discuss from a completely different angle. Quite often, we waste time arguing about ways of doing things. And while the discussion is necessary, we must also focus our efforts on actually doing what we spend so much time discussing. So it is imperative we understand while there are various methodologies to any given matter, my goal is to empower you to live your life intentionally BREATHING DEEP with every effort you execute.

To the reader, I will discuss with you various matters while consistently referencing Christian views. This fact does not mean people of other faiths cannot relate. All religions and theologies possess similar interpretations and some of them I will use in this book. However, for the Christian, I must equally forewarn you as well. What I say in this book may rub your convictions, traditions, and perspectives the wrong way. And I must honestly admit, I intend to! I intend to challenge what the preacher has preached to you and what you have learned in Bible study. My intentions are not to **harm** you but to **enhance** you. Quite often, in order to grow into something we need, it is necessary to realize what we do know possibly but not necessarily may be insufficient for where we want to be. It does not mean what we know is incorrect. It does not mean what we know lacks value.

What it does mean is we are traveling to a new place and not everything we know and the perspective thereof will sustain us in this new area of our lives. Therefore, we cannot say, "*I want to go to higher heights and deeper depths*" and simultaneously be of the mind to hold to our current perspectives with no room to enhance our frame of thought and even correct our reference of information, if there is an error. So before you engage in an inner emotional argument with the words on the page, take a moment, BREATHE DEEP, and consider the words I speak within the context I am speaking from. "*Be swift to hear, slow to speak, and slow to anger*".

To the theologian, *this book is not a religious apologetic.* I am not here to defend dogma or religious tradition. I am not here to pit Christianity against Islam, Hinduism against Taoism, Eastern tradition against Western Theology or the Baptist against the Pentecostal. While I will reference Bible Scriptures throughout this book and even discuss various biblical topics, events and characters, you must understand this one point; the conversation is brought to the table as an example of the principle in discussion or to set the stage for the next discussion. Therefore, as the effective practice of hermeneutics is to interpret Bible from the perspective of the author, I challenge you to do the same with this book and my words. If you fail to do so, you run the risk of misinterpreting what I am saying to you and the significance thereof.

Misinterpretation produces miscommunication. Miscommunication produces misdirected actions. Misdirected actions accumulate into *shallow* and *meaningless* lives. Do not allow your perspective to perpetuate a cycle you want so desperately to escape just to preserve your theological ego. Please govern yourself accordingly. Allow yourself the opportunity to see something you may never have seen or be enhanced by something you may already know.

This is a slow-read book because our lives are consummations of habits and behaviors, thoughts and experiences not to be handled lightly or carelessly. In this delicate process, there is a need to identify and challenge those experiences and perspectives in order to produce effective change. There are written exercises designed to have you engage your own experience and points of meditation constructed for you to contemplate your feelings and thoughts. They are in place to empower you to **STOP**, **BREATHE DEEP**, and **CONSIDER**. So take your time. You owe it to yourself to live your life the best way you can because it is the *ONLY* life on earth you will have. I am merely here to serve you as one of your many life coaches for the expressed intention of watching you blossom into the man or woman you were intended to be.

Let us now begin our journey together from a life of shallow and mediocre existence dictated by wounded perspectives and effortless actions to a new life; lived intentionally with meaning and depth sustained by fresh, solid, passionate convictions because we have decided to not just breathe, but BREATHE DEEP. Let us begin this journey to engage ourselves, wrestle ourselves, face ourselves, and change ourselves expecting and accepting nothing less than the best for ourselves.

CHAPTER 1

Give Me My Life Back
Building Your Platform

"I have come that you might have life and have it more abundantly"
John 10: 10 KJV

Breathing is one of the fundamental functions of human existence. If one does not breathe, one cannot live. Whether breathing by the strength of one's own lungs or an artificial respirator, breathing is a must. Breathing is such a vital phenomenon for us that our day-to-day health and productivity can be traced to how we breathe. Our ability to focus and be alert can (in part) be identified by assessing the flow of blood and oxygen in our bodies produced by our breathing patterns. Eastern religions such as Buddhism, Hinduism and Taoism (pronounced Dow-ism) teach, in meditation, the art of breathing. Releasing stress and negative energy by breathing is paramount to a clean essence. Martial arts such as Karate, Jujitsu, Tai Chi, and Tae Kwon Do teach how breathing affects performance and execution. Breathing is not just addressed in a literal sense but also it is literary. Entire books are titled on a single moment of emotional release like *"Waiting to Exhale"* and scriptures like *"And God breathed into him the breath of life and man became a living soul"*. There are even Christian theological courses on Pneumatology meaning "the study of the spirit". Quite often throughout the Bible spirit, wind, and breath are synonymous. Without question, Breathing is a foundation for life.

FOUNDATIONS

Foundations are pivotal to the stability of anything and everything. Whether a skyscraper or family values, the measure of success can always be traced to the foundations on which the success was built. A drug dealer's lifestyle has equal foundations as a preacher's lifestyle. The CEO's success has working foundations like a professional athlete. There are a series of events constantly occurring our lives. Those series of events create a context for us. Our individual but consistent responses to each context cultivate our overall perspective. We assign value to events, people, places, thoughts, words and even actions out of our context and perspective. Hence, everything we do hinges off of what we've previously experienced and the perspective thereof, which is the culmination of our responses. You are not as spontaneous as you think you are. There is a context and perspective you are operating from. Your ability to be argumentative is not just because you are that way. Behind the curtains of your life, there is context and perspective moving you. All of us communicate, live, and breathe particular contexts and perspectives influencing our every decision and action.

Context and perspective are parallel notions moving along the same continuum. They are inseparable and not negotiable. In order to understand and appreciate ourselves, it is necessary to understand how context and perspective influences us. Knowing our context and seeing our perspective for what it is (not trying to change our response yet) provides us with significant insight to not only the actions we may take but also why we may take the action as well. We will understand the significance of our concern because we will intentionally assess how we see life as we already unconsciously see it.

Before we can modify our lifestyles, it is vital we understand why our lifestyles are our lifestyles in the first place. If we make changes about our way of life now and fail to understand why we had that way in the first place, we are neglecting genuine growth. Furthermore, we run the risk of repeating the same cycle with our new lifestyles or potentially falling back to the way of life we just decided was not healthy for us. We are creating mirrors for ourselves. In this mirror, we will see us as we are. We will assess us, critique us, and modify us. Before we can change our perspective, we must understand and appreciate the point of view we currently have. At this point, we may not be ready to change our current perspective. However, we are ready to engage it.

What is "Context"? For the sake of this conversation, I will define context as, "*a past or present experience in our life*". It is a very simple definition and for good reason. First, these experiences aren't just isolated. There are factors making that situation the type of situation it may be. So when I speak of the experience, I also am including the factors as well. Secondly, these are the events and experiences in our lives that happened. They have occurred. They have come and gone. No matter how many times we rehearse the occurrences in our mind, it will happen the same way each time. They will have the same outcome. These events and experiences will play the same way every time we remember them because the events have happened and they can NEVER be changed. There is no magic to these moments. There are no special rewind buttons changing a single detail. Those moments are what those moments are. No matter how much we love them, how much we despise them, or how indifferent we may be towards them, those moments will never change their occurrences. They simply ARE.

What is "Perspective"? Since I have defined context as "*a past or present experience in our life*", I will define perspective as "***the culmination of our responses to the experiences in our life***". Perspective is our response to life totaled up. We didn't just wake up with perspective. Events happened to us and we responded. Another situation happened to us and we responded. Event after event happens and time after time we respond. Eventually, our responses develop into our perspective and our perspective governs our lives. We value everything off of our perspective. We hold conversations based off of our perspective. We recall stories from our perspectives. We reference our perspective in difficult times, decision times, and delightful times. While the events and experiences of our lives cannot be altered, the way we see them can be. So when it seems the experience has changed, it will never be the experience changing, just our outlook has changed.

One day 5 of us was watching the same Cleveland Indians' baseball game and all of us had a different version of the same game. Oftentimes, I wondered how could such a phenomenon happen. I discovered it was not the event itself we were merely recounting, but our perspective of the event as we recalled it. **It was our personal scope of sight for life we judged the game by.** We recounted the baseball game based off of the values we had. We talked about what was important to us. Since all 5 of us had different platforms of importance, our recollection of the baseball game would coincide with our inner platforms. We talked about what naturally mattered to us. One talked about the coaching because she felt it was the coaches' responsibility to prepare the team for the opponent. She was a basketball coach. My frat brother discussed the pitcher and catcher relationship. He was frustrated about the communication issues they were having throughout the entire game. Personally, he was married and the couple was working on better understanding and communicating to each other. An older gentleman saw the overall organization of the team. He liked how they moved as one. They covered their position well. They trusted each other. They knew where each other were. He was the Executive Director for a non-profit agency. One of my other boys critiqued the game, the players and how they performed. He felt some should be traded and some should retire. He was a sports agent for the NFL. All of us saw the same game. We argued about the same plays. We celebrated the same home runs. We threw our drinks down over the same strikeouts but the value of each event was on a different scale for each of us. When the Indians struck someone from Boston out my frat brother celebrated because the pitcher and catcher got the communication right while the Executive Director was happy the team was moving closer to the overall goal of winning the game. The coach and the sports agent became angry when the short stop dropped the ball. However, the coach's reason was she saw his lack of performance, as a failure to the coach for inadequately preparing his player for the type of batting style from the opposing player. The sports agent criticized the play because he felt the player was not athletically fit. All of us had cause to celebrate and criticize but our celebration and criticisms were steeped in perspective. We recounted the matters naturally meaningful to us.

You do the same. You see everything from your perspective. You value everything from your perspective. You judge everything from your perspective. The reference guide of life we frequently refer to is OUR PERSPECTIVE. Consequently, our perspective has significant impact on and in our lives. As I was the keynote speaker for the Citizenship Institute Awards ceremony in Cleveland, OH, I gave these words of admonition;

> "Let me warn you now, it is a DANGEROUS place to be in when others know more about you than you know about yourself. It is a dangerous place to be in when others have the inside scoop on you and you are completely oblivious to their insight on you. It is a dangerous place because when a person knows you better than you know yourself, they can maneuver you like a puppet on a string. They can position you as piece on a chest board for their on agendas with no regard for your well-being. You run the risk of being treated as a means to an end. You run the risk of becoming expendable. You are no longer treated as person but as a tool. And like all tools, they are only useful to us when we need them and when we don't need them; we throw them into the box until we need them again. And so is the case for many people used when they are not mindful of themselves. We run the risk and being used until there is no more need for us, and then we are thrown away until someone wants to use us again. So be mindful of yourself."

To not know your perspective or underestimate the power of perspective is to directly position yourself to be manipulated. It is the unwritten recipe for shallow existence. It is a direct invitation to be enslaved to a reality of powerlessness. We cannot take control of our life, we cannot make the most of our efforts, and we cannot fully appreciate our significance if we fail to comprehend our perspective and all that contributes to it. KNOW WHY YOU ARE THE WAY YOU ARE!

STOP!

BREATHE DEEP! & CONSIDER!

1. What are 2 experiences you have had and what has been your response to those experiences that now contribute to the way you see life?

2. How has your perspective of life affected your relationships and the way you communicate with other people?

3. Does your perspective make you more trusting of people or more suspicious? Why?

4. Can you see yourself developing a new response to your history? If so, how? If not, why?

Earlier I defined perspective as, "*the culmination of our responses to the experiences in our life*". It is precisely here, where we draw our 1st line in the sand. The difference between Breathing Deep and Dying Shallow is not only our response but also *HOW* we respond to our context. There are 2 ways and 2 ways only you and I can respond, directly or indirectly, intentionally or unintentionally. **Make no mistake about this point, no matter what happens to you in life's journey, you will respond to life.** It is inevitable and undeniable. The question is, "*will you respond to your life intentionally or unintentionally*". As mentioned before, you cannot change your context. The events have happened. They are unalterable. They are your history. It is your past. It is out of your control. Accept it. Did you hear me? ACCEPT IT! The more you fight an event that can never change, the longer YOU deny yourself the chance to get over it. The rape happened. The divorce happened. The death happened. The violence happened. The setback happened. You cannot change it. No matter how many times you pray about it, think about it, talk about it and even deny it, the truth is…*IT HAPPENED AND IT WILL NEVER CHANGE*! ACCEPT IT!

I am not speaking as a man so cavalier about something so delicate and fragile. I thoroughly understand the difficulty of coming to grips with something I never wanted to happen to me in the first place. It can be a depressing place. It can be a frustrating place. Yes my friend, it can even be an angry and lonely place. How do you say what you feel when there are no words to adequately express your sadness? Who can you talk to about something so humiliating it makes you sick to your stomach and you vomit at the very thought of it? These experiences are the things that make us want to crawl in bed and never wake up. These are the events that make us want to hide under a rock and never come out. These are the situations making us want to kill ourselves or kill others. And we mean, "*kill*" in every sense of the word. We are not speaking of a literary ending of something abstract. We are not discussing a figurative conclusion of a general idea. WE WANT BLOOD! WE WANT REVENGE! WE WANT JUSTICE! We do not care about the psychoanalytical babble of people divorced from our experience. We do not want advice from people untouched by the pain of what really happened to us. We need someone to understand our emotions. We need someone to relate to our plight. We need someone to feel what we feel and how we feel it. We need a connection. We need a bond.

What people fail to understand is when we start talking like this; we have not lost our sanity. We are not beside ourselves. We do not need to be sedated. It is our emotions speaking. It is our feelings being vented. Rationale and logic do not have any authority with us when it comes to crimes, which have been committed against us. Whether personally, physically, sexually, socially, emotionally, professionally, religiously, etc, we do not care what makes sense! We have not abandon what is right and what is wrong. We have not turned our backs to the law. But what we are saying is that while the law may punish the action what punishes the crimes against the heart? Who holds court for the violations of our soul? Who hands out the sentence for our feelings? Who are the jury members convening regarding the infractions of the soul? These are the questions we ask which rarely get answered. And more often than not, we are given even more unsatisfactory answers when one tries.

Nonetheless my friend, as justified as we are in our stand for crimes committed against us, sooner or later, we *STILL* must come to grips that IT HAPPENED. We cannot change it. You cannot go back in time and alter it. It happened. It hurts but happened. You have cried and you may be crying now but it happened. You may hate it with a fire few can empathize with but it happened. There is no easy way to say this my friend; you *MUST* accept it for what it is and move forward. To deny it happened positions you with a perspective self-destructive. On one hand, you are steadily attempting to deceive yourself. On the other, you are becoming full of anger and bitterness because it is not working and you know it. Why fight this unnecessary battle? There are plenty of other battles you will need to fight? Save your energy. Save yourself the stress. Enough fighting. Enough denial. Accept it. Embrace it. Engage it and move forward!

While we may not have been in control of the experiences in our lives, we do control how we respond to those experiences. So control your perspective. People who allow their events and experiences to dictate what they will feel and how they will think are only setting themselves up for a shallow existence. They are not in control of their life. Life controls them. They are meandering through life unintentionally. Every problem will be someone else's fault. Every disappointment will be someone else's doing. Every event will be labeled "out of their control". And they will be absolutely right because they failed to TAKE control. BREATHE DEEP! BE ON PURPOSE! LIVE INTENTIONALLY! While there will be plenty of events out of our control, every event is NOT. Look at your life. Remember those events. Take deep breaths as you wrestle with coming to grips with what happened. Accept it. Develop a fresh way of seeing it. ***Always remember, there is always more than one angle to a good snapshot!*** Come up out of tunnel vision and see life on a broader scope. See more than yourself. See more than your experience. See more than what happened to you. Can my tragic experience be an asset to another? Can my disappointment be an encouragement to another? If it can, then my experience can still have good value after all! If I can reconcile my sad moments as an experience investment in the lives of others, then I can see my life having a renewed significance. Can you hear yourself saying that to yourself? Can you hear yourself cheering you on to push past the disappointment for the sake of not only yourself but also for someone else who needs to know what you know? And they may never know what you know if you don't accept what happened to you and tell them how you made it through to have peace. People need you to make it. Children need you to get past this so you can help them do the same. Colleagues need you to overcome this obstacle. Spouses need you to conquer this issue so they can love you without suspicion. You need this so you can breathe easy once again. So do it! ***Never forget, our lives MUST count for more than a catalogue of memories.***

STOP!

BREATHE DEEP! & CONSIDER!

1. What are 3 experiences in your life you have a difficult time accepting happened to you?

2. For each experience, what crime was committed against your heart, your body, your faith, your trust etc causing so much pain to make you want to deny it ever happened?

3. Was your response to each event then out of anger or out of sadness?

4. Is your perspective now bitter, hateful, skeptical, and cynical?

5. Can you see someone being enhanced by your experience if you can find the strength to share it with a hopeful insight?

How do foundations work? How do they support structures? What is the correlation between structures under the building compared to structures above ground? Is there a difference between the types of material used? I pose these questions because these are only a few concerns architects and engineers wrestle with in the development and construction of any given design. In a similar process, we must raise some serious inquiry to ourselves concerning our foundations. One of the many questions we must ask ourselves is, *"Can our foundation adequately support our dreams"*.

An example of foundations equipped to support success will be a young man who is a successful street life thug. Yes, this is negative lifestyle but a lifestyle our kids desire to emulate. Therefore, it is a lifestyle we should evaluate as some of our very own children desire to pursue it. The street life success is not exclusive action but combinations of other factors as well. His experiences (context) and his developed responses to those experiences (perspective) have conditioned him to **think** and **behave** a certain way. He does not process information the same way as others. Where others see a dead end, he sees his empire extended. His foundations provide him with the necessary tools to not only survive but also live; and live abundantly on the streets. He is not satisfied with living paycheck to paycheck. He wants more. He needs more. He demands more. His appetite is insatiable. He looks to capitalize on every circumstance. Where a novice may flip $100 to $500, he can flip $100 to $5000. He does not waste his time with people who talk much but produce little. He removes them. He is not intimidated by challenges. He engages them. He does not fear obstacles. He moves around them. He creates sources of revenue where poverty exists. His vitality motivates others. Those in his shadows model his work ethic. He understands the streets. He understands emotions will get you killed. He comprehends his life is fragile but understands the exposure of such a reality will self-destruct his kingdom. His history has prepared him for his future. His foundations are substantial to support his dreams, if his dreams coincide with his past. He is empowered to take on any challenge. He maximizes his opportunities and where there are no opportunities, he creates them.

Now while I must confess the lifestyle of a street thug or hustler I do not condone, I respect his effort and admire it equally the same. I respect it because he's true to his conviction. His mind, his heart and his body move as one. He's committed to what he believes. His perspective may be misguided but it's creating tangible results. Who can deny such a display? Whether we like the lifestyle or not, it's a real lifestyle nonetheless using these very principles, to manifest its desires and dreams. People model themselves after him not because he has money only, but the attitude on the streets is "money is power". He who has the money has the power. Influence. Freedom. Nice cars. Sexy Women. The ability to make law keepers go crooked and the ability to make preachers change their sermons are just some of the results when drug dealers press their power. He has demonstrated how context and perspective can make the difference in the outcome of a pursued venture. Just think, how awesome it would be if you and I translated such ambition, focus, and execution to our plans as a street hustlers, thugs, and pimps do on the streets. I reiterate this is not a celebration of this lifestyle but recognition of the effort it takes to create such a tangible and desirable reality. His emotions, his intellect, his sexuality, his world view were all the results of his developed perspective as his direct response to past contexts which have now become the foundations of his life. Our lives are built on perspectives and these perspectives have now become our foundations. NO ONE IS EXEMPT FROM THAT REALITY! ABSOLUTELY NO ONE!

REMEMBERING YOUR DREAMS

It is necessary for me to take a look at very a delicate matter. It is the matter of our dreams. I start here because all of us, including myself, have had dreams. As children we were urged to dream. The idea behind pushing us to dream is that we would have some direction for our life. Dreaming ignites a power within humanity to create. It is the notion dreams will propel us into life with confidence of achieving our dreams because we were creative enough to dare to dream. Therefore, dreaming was as important to our natural development as children as arithmetic, writing, and reading. To deny a child the opportunity to dream and play out those dreams is to deny the same child the opportunity to develop into the man or woman he/she could become. So whether we choose to have dreams now or whether we have stopped dreaming altogether, at some point in our lives; we all have dreamed.

Allow me take the opportunity to transition into what my dreams were (as a teenager) to paint a more vivid picture of the point I'm attempting to make. Walk with me down memory lane for a moment or two just to see how vital pursuing dreams really can be.

When the movie "*Boomerang*" starring Eddie Murphy, Robin Givens, and Halle Berry came out, I dreamed of having the apartment, the office and the lifestyle of Eddie Murphy. I looked up to the man and his character in the movie. I liked how he walked into the office and the women salivated after him. I enjoyed the look of his office with all the colors and the various designs of furniture and artwork on the walls. I admired how this Black man had such freedom in his schedule whereby he could come and go as he pleased. It was appealing to me he was in charge of his life. He was the creative mastermind making results and receiving the praise. I liked how he had a staff. People answered to him. He had power. He could fire someone or hire someone. He decided how much people would be paid, if they worked for him. I liked the man's suits. I wanted his clothes. I wanted the baby grand piano in his apartment. I liked the friendships he had with Martin Lawrence and Alan Greer. I wanted the king size bed he had. I wanted to travel like he traveled staying in hotels and flying on airplanes from one place to another. But there was a problem. I was only in the 10th grade.

Girls were not salivating over me. I played basketball and while I was good, I was not the sexy man in school. My parents had a piano but it was not black and shiny like Eddie Murphy's, it was white with chipped paint, out of tune keys, and other keys broken. It stood against the wall and blended with my parents furniture while my mom's plants sat on top of the piano. I wanted the stereo system Eddie Murphy had but all my parents had was a record/tape player and I had no tapes. I wanted to play the new songs like Toni Braxton's *Love Should have Brought You Home Last Night* and Babyface's *Whip Appeal* but all my parents had were records like Midnight Star's *No Parking on the Dance Floor* and Atlantic Starr's *Secret Lovers*. I thought about going into my dad's van and borrowing some of his smooth jazz tapes so I could pretend being like Eddie Murphy but I knew he would give me the royal Bufford Introduction of my rear-end to his belt (an introduction I had many times over), if he found out that I had his tapes. And then I liked how Eddie Murphy had his own place but I lived with my parents, my sisters, and PeeWee, my dog.

To live like Eddie Murphy was my dream but my present status looked nothing like what I wanted. I knew it would take a lot of work to get there and I had no clue of knowing where to begin. I wanted women to desire me. I wanted to come and go as I pleased without having to ask my parents at the risk of hearing them tell me "*No*". I wanted to be in control of my life. I wanted to work out of my own office but instead I worked cutting grass in the neighborhood to make an honest buck. I wanted to be in a suit and smell good. I wanted to wear the nicest colognes but cutting grass did not make me feel this way. I did not feel that I was sexy. I felt foolish. And it was so humiliating when the girls walk down the street and saw me, they laughed. I didn't have this intriguingly sculpted physique but I was skinny. And my parents made me wear these glasses so I could see better but I thought they were ugly. Not to mention, I smelled funky. I didn't smell good with the nice smelling fragrances for men but I "stanked". I "stanked" real bad. I smelled like hot grass mixed with oil and gasoline on top of a whole lot of funk. That was so not sexy (and believe me when I say I tried). And I wanted to be like Eddie Murphy, sexy! However, where I was in life was much different from where I wanted to be. And that single reality was enough to make me frustrated enough whereby I disengaged the present world (as I saw it) and I began living as if I lived in the world where I could be who I wanted to be. MY PERSPECTIVE CHANGED AND MY BEHAVIOR FOLLOWED!

On Friday nights after BET's Video Soul top 20 videos with Donnie Simpson went off, I would make sure my family was sleep and I would pretend I was grown like Eddie Murphy. I would get in my mom's "88 Grand Am and pretend I was driving to an office party. I never started the car because I knew my father (who was a police officer) would think someone was trying to steal the car and he would beat me until I died or I wished death upon me. So I turned the ignition just enough where I could hear *"For Lovers' Only"* with Bobby Rush on 93 FM WZAK in Cleveland, OH. I would walk in the house and while no one was there but me, I imagined a house full of people. I turned on the music as if a DJ was spinning the music. My parents were used to me being up late on the weekends so they slept through the night. I lived in that world for 3 years.

And here's something we need to take note of. Someone could very easily say I was just playing pretend. And I would say to that person that they were right. But what people fail to understand is there is power in playing pretend because we are acting out what we want to become. We're expanding our creative power to see what is beyond our eyes. And that simple action is enough to make us want our desires to be more than just acting. We want that life to be a reality. Playing pretend makes the dream all the more real and brings it just a little closer to home because we can see it so much clearer that we are now acting as if we're there though we're not there yet. Our dreams are giving us definite direction. When we played pretend as kids, we built the reality we wanted in the midst of the reality we didn't. When we play pretend as adults, our current behavior is as if what is to be is already now. When we play pretend, tomorrow is today and today is yesterday. *Therefore, since playing pretend is a game we all played as children, playing pretend is really the natural practice of faith in action because faith calls that which is not as though it already is! And thus it follows we behave according to our expectation and not to our current situation.* What we see changed. We no longer saw where we were but we saw where we wanted to be and we behaved accordingly. Our response changed and the more our responses changed, the more our perspective developed and grew. My friend, playing pretend as a child was our 1st encounter with naturally practicing having faith for a life we didn't have yet. Playing pretend was our 1st experience in believing in our dreams and CHANGING OUR PERSPECTIVE!

When I graduated from Buchtel High School in Akron, OH in '95, I thought life would be like my dream world. It was not the case. After never being suspended a day in my life from school, I was expelled from World Harvest Bible College in Columbus, OH in less than 1 year. Bishop H. E. Bellinger and Mt. Sinai Holy Temple (now Cathedral of the Covenant) in Columbus, OH paid my entire spring semester bill and I was kicked out of college 4 days later. They could not get a refund either. I was so humiliated I refused to go home. I could not bring myself to face my pastor, the church or my family because I let so many people down. I could not look Bishop Bellinger in his face after knowing they paid money for me to go to school and I was kicked out 96 hours later. I lost my job due to depression. I went to temp agencies to find work but had no car, no money to ride the bus to get to a job and so I found myself being very poor. I stayed with my boy Jerome for a couple of months but ran up his phone bills and almost wrecked a friendship that was keeping me sane. My best friend, Tony, who graduated from Buchtel a year before I did, tried his best to encourage me but I was so overwhelmed with sadness his advice fell on deaf ears. I was a wreck and I was wrecking everything around me. The world I dreamed of was not the world I was in. Even after I left the world that I thought was so bad, the new dream I was living was still not my dream at all. It was nightmare. The more I tried to hold to my dreams, the more my reality seemed to overpower my desires until my dreams came crashing down all around me and I did not know what to do.

One of the most frustrating experiences people can ever have is dreaming dreams that never happen as planned. All of us have had dreams. All of us have had aspirations and desires. Some of us have dreams of marriage. We dream of a happy marriage unlike the marriages around us filled with vice and conflict. We dream of being content and loving each other and not worried if our marriage will fail. But we become devastated when our dreams shatter in our hands and what we feared so much has now manifested and we feel helpless to stop it. As men, there is nothing like having the dream of being adequately equipped to support our families where our wives and kids will not have to want for anything only to have tragedy strike and we lose our ability to provide for them. Suddenly, our kids are in need. Our wives are stressed and worried. We are angered that our most sincere efforts are foiled to make our dreams a reality. Dreams are so potent they have the ability to push us through life's toughest times. They have the power fueling drives we didn't know existed within us. Dreams ignite fire within us in ways the greatest inspirational speaker could never tap. Dreams are like adrenaline. When the situation requires extra push, we can count on our hunger for our dreams to pull us through. But when we allow life to shatter our dreams, life is a different place. The songs we once hummed we can no longer remember their melodies. The passion we once had becomes ghost. Our excitement dissipates. Our glow fades. And we feel empty. We feel shallow. We feel hollow. Our strength, our drive, our vitality, it's all gone. We are left feeling helpless. We are left feeling powerless. We are left with pieces of something we desire so much and no clue how to achieve it. Like I was at 19 years old, we are left with broken dreams, plenty of questions, more anger, and no answers.

However, what we cannot afford to do is to allow our dreams to die. **For the secret to life is that life has to mean MORE than what has happened to us.** Our lives cannot just be a summary of past events. Our lives must mean more. Our lives must count for more than a catalogue of memories. Our dreams may have been shattered. We may not have accomplished what we dreamed of becoming. We may be left with nothing more than broken expectations, fractured hopes, and pieces of dreams. However, do you not realize there is not a single building, cathedral, or mansion not made from pieces? There is no house in existence built from anything perfect. Everything was built from pieces. Pieces of steal, iron, brick, mortar, carpet, wood and more contributes to some of the most beautiful structures known to humanity. Some of the ancient structures of yesteryear are appraised at a higher value than whole structures. Do you not know there is something to be said about the pieces remaining in your life? The pieces remaining are a testimony to the strength of your dreams. They are not a failure. You are justified in the pain you felt from the disappointment of shattered expectations. You are within your right to cry over the sadness of what happened to you. Your pain is real. Your frustrations are real. Yes, even your anger and rage are real and justified. You are vindicated in your feelings on the matter of the brokenness of your dreams.

Nonetheless, your perspective, which is your response, is completely YOUR CHOICE!!! So I urge you to guard your dreams! The world is an aggressive place. Life can be cruel, callous and indifferent. People can be inconsiderate, jealous and vindictive. And if you are not careful with your dreams, life will bring events with the ability to kill your dreams, if you let them. The world will take your most precious dreams and stump them under foot and never stop to see if you will be alright. People will smash your dreams against the rocks of their failure and cause you to be shipwrecked as they are. They will abuse your dreams until you abandon them. They will harass your dreams until you hate them. They will violate your dreams until you forsake them. Life can get so hard that if you are not careful, you will grab the knife and castrate your own dreams ability to bring you life. Tragedy will happen. Disappointments will occur. Your dreams will be injured. Your hopes will be violated. Your aspirations will be raped. And during those moments, hopelessness will attempt to seize your vulnerability, gripping your dreams by the throat choking the very life out of it. Fear will incarcerate your dreams suffocating it in the prison of powerlessness.

And yes, your dreams may have already been shattered. And while there are no easy answers to address this matter, nonetheless, there is still an answer for this too. As difficult is it will be, as challenging as it will feel, and as disheartening as the situation is, you must get down on your hands and knees, gather the pieces and start again. I know it is sad. I know it makes you cry. I know it even makes you angry. But you cannot allow your dreams to die!!! Your dreams may be shattered. They may be shattered to little pieces. But you must NEVER LET YOUR DREAMS DIE!

You can wallow in your misery and blame everyone in the world for what happened to you or you can realize the significance of the pieces that made it and use those pieces to build your platform. You may not have been in control of what happened to you then but YOU CAN TAKE CONTROL OF YOUR LIFE NOW! At least you know with these pieces, they can take a beating and keep the structure up. These pieces, which have made it, are the pieces that have proven themselves through the test of time. These parts of your dreams could not be killed because your marriage failed. These pieces could not be destroyed because of the rape. These pieces could not be forgotten because you started a family sooner than you expected. As a matter of fact, you are reading this book right now because you want to know is there any value to these pieces and how do you use them to start again. Yes, we need dramatic words and actions to shake us out of apathy. **Therefore, I am challenging you right here and right now! You can maintain the same perspective you have had all these years and receive the same results you have always had or you can make a new response today and develop a fresh perspective now**! If you are to build your platform, you will need those pieces. If you are to have a strong foundation, you will need the stuff, which has proven its durability through the test of pain, sadness and setbacks. Do not allow your pain to cause you to forget your desires. If you have decided your life has to mean more than what it currently is, TAKE A DEEP BREATH AND REMEMBER YOUR DREAMS!!!

STOP!

BREATHE DEEP! & *CONSIDER!*

1. Remember 2 of your dreams, what were they?

2. Are your dreams fulfilled, in development, or shattered? What happened?

3. What are your dreams like now or do you dream at all?

4. Can you find the courage to dream again?

ASSESSING MY INVENTORY

Before we start building our platform we must take inventory. Taking inventory is significant because it allows us to see what we are working with. It allows us to assess the value of our goods, the strength of our product and it gives us a 1st hand look at what is ready for the public's eye and what is damaged and what needs to be thrown away. Taking inventory also prepares us for what we need that we do not already have. Since our contexts and perspectives constitute our foundations on which we build our lives, it is time we get personal. This part is always hard for us to do because the point of conversation and investigation is not someone else. We become our own focus. We take a look at how awesome we are and simultaneously assess how awful we are too. However, the value of such a practice enables us to see precisely where we are. Knowing the ground we stand on now is equally important as knowing where we want to be   And it is the understanding of where we are in our personal lives preparing us to build a platform for where we want to be.

1.   Dreams

We have just talked about remembering your dreams. Our dreams are important because they are part of our inventory. Dreams serve the purpose of direction. Whether long-term or short term, dreams take us out of current circumstance and place us in better conditions, specifically ideal conditions. Your dreams are essential to your success. They are the stars in life's night sky, which you will navigate your entire life according to. Your dreams will serve you as your guide. When you are lost along life's journey, when you are confused, when you are frustrated, your dreams will usher you back to your course. Your dreams will always keep your focus, your mind, and your heart above the mess you are currently in. Your dreams are precious. They are valuable. They are necessary.

Hence, this may be one of the reasons why we sometimes experience frustrations. For many of us, we have stopped dreaming. Consequently, we feel our lives are not going anywhere. We feel like we are not moving. We are putting effort into projects and we are frustrated with the lack of progress. We feel we are wasting our time. And the more we try to make miracles out of mess, the more frustrated we become when the mess gets messier. Not only is our effort limited to projects but people also. Whether platonic, business or intimate, relationships are very taxing endeavors. We invest ourselves in our relationships. We give our best in relationships. We fight to be honest when it is easier to tell a lie. We wrestle with keeping our word when it is more convenient to break our promise. We struggle to maintain fidelity when it is more exciting to indulge in temptation. And after we battle against doing what is wrong to do what is right, we feel the payoff does not equal the effort or the energy we expended. We have forgotten our dreams. For many of us, we've allowed our life's experiences to rob us of the fire of chasing our dreams. There is nothing like sacrificing what you planned to do for yourself in order to make time for someone else and he/she is the least bit appreciative of your effort. Or there is nothing that can get under the skin of the person who has taken time to cook for the person he/she loves and that person goes to McDonald's when a fresh home cooked meal is at home waiting for him/her.

It is situations like these driving a person to wonder. I wondered how did I get here. I questioned myself as to why I was experiencing this. I realized one answer was I had forgotten my dreams. I got away from what I wanted. If you are like me, the situations I mentioned are not unfamiliar to you. Like me, you may be guilty of the same thing. You may have forgotten your dreams. You may have gotten away from pursuing the type of relationship you want to settle for the present but temporary convenience of shallow romance. You may have laughed or screamed at the book as you read the words. I was thinking of several women in my past as I wrote and I even remember how I felt when the situations happened. I was furious. I was enraged. I said to myself over and over again, *"I'm done with those type of women"*. It disgusted me to know I was investing in women who were taking everything I had to give and yet, never took time to reciprocate in their own way. Now I'm not a high maintenance guy to say the least. However, everyone deserves to have someone who will make him or her feel special not because we are keeping score. We deserve someone who will make us feel special because they want to make us feel special.

However, when we reset our priorities according to our dreams, we will become adamant about refusing to settle for less than what is best. The day is over for begging people to be with us. Either you want us or you don't but we are no longer begging. We have too much to live for. We have too much to accomplish. We do not have time to waste with leech mentalities. These are the people who believe they will live their lives off of our success. Some of us need to grab the knife and cut them off of our skin. There are others with crab attitudes. These folks are always trying to pull us down when we try to get out of the barrel. These two mentalities are deadly to building our platform. And one of the ways to avoid such entrapments is chasing our dream.

Our dreams not only act as a night light in dark places, it is our standard for which we measure everything against. Many of the situations I just mentioned could be avoided if we use our dreams as a standard, not merely a point of destination. Our dreams must reflect where we want to be, not where we are. Remember as kids we played pretend. Whatever was our standard for the character we played, that's how we behaved. It's the same for pursuing our dreams. If our dreams reflect where we are, then our life will go nowhere. The only movement we will have is reoccurring drama with reoccurring emotions happening with the same type of people producing the same type of results. Our dreams must be bigger than what we have and much more extensive than what we know.

When I taught a workshop at New Bethel Baptist Church in Youngstown, OH, we broke out into small groups and I posed a question; "*What is the difference between a swamp and a river*". A young lady in her early 20's attending Kent State University said, "*Water displacement*". When I asked her to explain she replied, "*In a swamp, the water is everywhere. As a result, water cannot move because it is everywhere. Hence, the water becomes stagnant and what is considered having the ability to bring life, it does exactly the opposite bringing death. However, a river is different altogether. A river has water moving. Because the water is moving, it has the ability to produce life. As a result, life flourishes around rivers while death looms around swamps*". I smiled and was thoroughly delighted to hear her answer, so I posed one more question, "*What does a river have to make the water move that swamps do not have*"? And after some discussion, the same woman spoke and said, "*Banks control the water in the river. They are what keep the water in the river and what protects everything else from falling in the river*". And she was precisely correct. The banks of a river control not only the water, but also how the water flows. The river's banks can control how fast or slow the water moves. The height of the bank can indicate when the water is at a critical flood level. The banks are the standard for measuring the river. Hence, the banks have the ability to harness the power of the river.

Our dreams are the banks in our rivers of life. Our dreams are the standards for living. We can gauge what we need to do by taking note of our dreams. Our dreams make demands of us. Since our dreams should be more than what we have and more than what we know, we must modify our current lifestyle to position us to reach what we are dreaming of. If you want to be a fashion model, it makes no sense for you to enroll in every pie-eating contest. The lifestyle of fashion models has a different demand than not being a fashion model. If you want the fashion model lifestyle, then the changes must take place now in order to position you to achieving your dream. If you want to be in the Olympics, you cannot spend every weekend in the clubs getting drunk. An Olympian needs to train constantly. And their training requires their full attention, time and energy. You cannot believe you can spend your time out late habitually and believe your performance will be excellent. On the same par, your eating habits must coincide with demands of your desire. A high performance vehicle cannot execute a high performance demonstration while its constantly being fueled with low performance gasoline. We must conform our lives to the dream we are pursuing. Like banks to a river, dreams are the standard with which we must govern our lives according to. To do anything less is futile, shallow, and worthless.

I cannot tell you the number of women I speak to on a daily basis and they dream of having a "good" man. When we have these conversations and I ask them, "*What are you doing to position yourself for a good man*", you wouldn't believe some of the answers I get. Some have said they pay attention to what their horoscopes say. Some say they should not have to position themselves, a "good man" should find them. Others quote the verse in Proverbs, "*He that findeth a wife, findeth a good thing*". And yet there are others who have responded saying nothing. It amazes me these women and countless others want something so specific but fail to take direct action to attaining it. We must adopt the perspective, behavior, and habits of our dreams now. To not do so, incapacitates us to ever reach what we so desperately dream. This kind of action positions us for shallow existences. Now while there is no single formula for successfully securing a "good man or woman", like the rest of dreams, there are intentional questions we can ask which produce very direct actions we can take:

- What are my needs?

    Most people look at relationships in regards to the other person first. How does he/she look? How does he/she dress? What kind of job do they have? How much money do they make? Rarely, do we take time to look at what we need for us first. Not to dismiss physical attraction or sexual chemistry, we must ask some preliminary questions before anyone ever catches our eye. What is my lifestyle like? What demands does my life make on me? What potential demands will my lifestyle make on others romantically involved with me? What type of person do I need for my type of lifestyle?

- What are my dreams?

I have asked this question in the STOP-BREATHE DEEP-CONSIDER section. It is important to look at this question again here. Our lives are chartered according to the stars of our dreams. So know your dreams! It is a sure recipe for chaos and disaster to invite someone into your life or mine when they do not have the capacity of seeing our dreams and helping us work towards them. GUARD YOUR DREAMS.

To know where we are in our lives and to know where we want to be positions us for a meaningful life. Our dreams give us the direction for where we want to be and help guide us in effectively building our platform. Therefore, we must guard our dreams.

2. Personal Strengths

This is the part of our inventory most of us are aware of. We like this part of ourselves. It is precisely our strengths and natural abilities giving us a sense of security and esteem about ourselves. Our strengths give us personal value and self worth. Our strengths give us an edge over people who do not have what we have or who cannot naturally do what we do at the drop of a hat with little to no effort.

If we are to be successful in building our platform and

establishing our foundations, we must know our strengths. Let us define what strength really is. Keeping the definition simple **strength** is, "*our ability to do and do well*". These are the things we are good at. We can do them and we do them well. It is the gifts, abilities, talents, and natural aptitudes for success within every single one of us. Our strengths separate us from other people. Our strengths distinguish us from other efforts. Therefore, we must know our strengths. You must know what natural aptitudes you possess. What do you do naturally well? What do you do excellent without a considerable amount of thinking? What flows up out of you when you are in the shower, when you are driving your car, when you are sitting quietly on the toilet? What melody crosses your lips? What thought crosses your mind? What concept do you ponder? What notions do you wrestle with making a reality? These are the questions we must ask to discover our strengths.

Many of us believe we know our strengths very well. But the question is, "*do we*". I ask this because we thought we understood our perspectives about life until I challenged it earlier in the chapter. We think we are so secure with the information we have until someone shows us that we do not know as much as we credit ourselves with. It is human nature to look for the evidence that justifies our already preconceived suspicions. People are guilty in our eyes and we naturally look for evidence to reinforce it. As much as we would like to credit ourselves with being open to the possibility of error, for many of us, we do not believe such a notion exists and thus our behavior follows our first inclination, which was our only inclination in the first place. I call this "*self-prosecution*". Self-Prosecution is "*when we have convinced ourselves of the validity of our own argument*". We become the judge, the jury and the executioner. The problem is the only evidence presented is our own suspicions and baseless assumptions. So naturally, if we feel we know our strengths, it also naturally follows we will not seek to know our strengths better because we feel we already know them. And if we do not know our strengths (as we already think we do), then we will never know our strengths until someone shows us the contrary.

An example of this was when I moved to Cleveland as the new District Executive for the Boy Scouts of America. I was new to the city and unfamiliar with the geographical outline of my district. I had a colleague who had a district north of mine. He said his district ended and mine began on a certain street. I disagreed with him. He said he knew the city better than I did as well as he knew my district better than I did. I told him he was wrong. He did not listen. I got frustrated. We took it to the director. He was no help. We went back and forth for a couple of months until I finally went to the city planning commission and had a friend draft up a map. When she did, I brought the map to my director and colleague and it was clearly stated I was correct. My colleague felt he already knew the city and he felt no need to rehearse his knowledge to see if he was in error because he was sure he already knew what he was talking about. It was only until I had proof to the contrary from someone outside our organization that knew the area better than he did to verify what I, as the new guy, had been saying all along. Only after I had outstanding, undeniable proof, did my colleague change his mind.

You are the single most important person in your life. Everything you do will have all sorts of impact on people near and around you but no one will be as impacted as you. You live with you. You face you. You wrestle with you. Therefore, since you have such an influence and impact concerning you, you must know your strengths. Question your strengths. Challenge your strengths. Do not just assume because you have done something all of your life that you know why you do it so well. Discover the reasons why you do something so well. Even if you think you already know, look again. Make sure the knowledge you have about yourself is sure knowledge and not assumed presumptions. What you do with yourself is an indication of what you will do to others. Do right by yourself. Take time with yourself. Engage yourself. Know what you know and be sure what you know is correct. This is you we are talking about. These are your strengths we are talking about. Know them. Know how they work. Know how they developed. Know how to improve them. You need them to get you to your dreams. You need them to take you to the next level. It is imperative you know your strengths.

3.   Personal Weaknesses

The thought of our weakness is not a thought building self-esteem unlike the thoughts of our strengths. In all actuality, it does the exact reverse. If our strengths give us confidence then our weaknesses robs us of the same. If we celebrate our strengths, our weaknesses are what embarrass us. Our weaknesses are fragile, delicate, and quite sensitive. I have seen grown men cry, egos evaporate, and facades crumble when weaknesses are exposed. What are weaknesses? As I defined strengths as "*our abilities to do and do well*", I must equally define **weaknesses** as "***our inabilities to do and not do well***". However, weaknesses are just as essential to assessing our inventory as our dreams and strengths are. Regardless of their fragility, weaknesses are necessary to our success. This may sound abstract and extremely weird but we need our weaknesses to have meaningful and fulfilling lives. What makes the difference is our perspective concerning our weaknesses. Yes, our weaknesses many times, empower us to BREATHE DEEP.

There is a secret to weakness. Perspective is everything. How we see our weaknesses will determine how valuable it is to us and our perspective will determine how well we utilize its reality. ***The secret is this: weaknesses are invitations for people to support you.*** Yes my friend, our weaknesses with the right perspective are invitations for support we thought we could never receive. As a child, my grandmother told me, *"the Good Lord made us with strengths to let us know we could reach our dream and the Good Lord made us with weaknesses to remind us we couldn't do it without him"*. What my grandmother was teaching me at an early age was weaknesses are not a human deficiency but a human necessity. The reality is we are made with both. Strengths and weaknesses. This is the beauty of being human. We have such a capacity to overcome any obstacle and wrestle any challenge simultaneously we can fall apart at any time. How awesome of a contradiction we live with. We are such a beautiful people because we have such a capacity to be strong and at the same time so weak and fragile. We are not successful because we have no fears. We are not accomplished because we have no areas of improvement. We push and push hard because we believe. We believe in something that transcends our lack of abilities. We believe in something that outdoes our lack of resources. Our convictions and our perspectives are so much stronger than our strengths and our weaknesses combined. And yet we still have weaknesses. Wow, my friend, you and I are truly an awesome phenomenon.

When I visited my parents for the holidays, my family and friends watched Superman IV. After the movie, we got into a discussion about Superman. As I listened and engaged in the conversation, I recognized while we may celebrate and want to be like Superman and laugh at Clark Kent, it is Clark Kent we can identify with. It is Clark Kent stumbling, stuttering, getting yelled at by the boss, and going to work. It is Clark Kent dealing with annoying colleagues, paying bills, missing the cab, forever being ignored and constantly underestimated. Superman is the ideal reality but Clark Kent is the practical reality. Clark Kent is where we live and who we really are. Only when Superman comes in contact with kryptonite, can we relate to him. We can relate to Superman because he is experiencing weakness and we see it. All of us know we have weaknesses in theory, but only until we experience weakness do we want to do something about them. We must change the way we perceive our weakness, if we are to breathe deep in life.

The story of Adam and Eve is a very popular story. Many have used this story on countless occasions to argue the validity and justification of their argument. Preachers have used this story to justify a patriarchal society. Men have argued that humanity is filled with vice because of women's deception. Many men claim women are a man's kryptonite. The story is used as an explanation why women experience pain in labor. Violence, poverty, hunger, and disease exist in the world because Adam and Eve sinned against God. And while there are many more examples of using this biblical story as reasons for what is happening in the world, I will also use this story in a similar fashion to make my argument clear.

God creates Adam. Adam lives in a perfect world. Adam experiences perfection with every breath, with every step, with every word, and with every blink. Adam is surrounded by perfection. Adam, himself, is a perfect human being. There is no flaw within Adam. Everything he does is perfect. Everything he touches will be perfection. Every thought process is perfected. However, he is perfect and still found lacking. Adam is perfect but still found insufficient. Adam is perfect and still had WEAKNESS. Now the weakness I speak of is not the weaknesses due to his ability to sin. That reality was never a weakness. It was a choice. Adam chose to transgress. The weakness I mention is Adam's inability to do. Remember strength is defined as "*our ability to do and do well*" and weakness is "*our inability to do and not do well*". There was something Adam could not do and do it well. There was something needing to be done which Adam could not fulfill completely by himself. What was the task Adam had to accomplish whereby he was insufficiently equipped to successfully accomplish? The answer is the mandate God gave humanity in Chapter 1 saying, "*be fruitful, multiply, replenish the earth, subdue it, and have dominion over it*". Adam could not do this by himself. The charge was bigger than the resources Adam was equipped with. So the reality was while Adam was perfect, his perfection did not make him all sufficient. There were things Adam simply could not do. He had a weakness. And Adam needed help.

So you have God go on record saying, "*I will make an* **Help Meet** (for Adam)". This is truly a significant turn in the story. Now we have the introduction of a new character. Not only do we have her introduction but also we know her significance even before she arrives on the scene. She is coming in the story to help Adam where Adam could not help himself. She is not inferior to Adam. She is not a subordinate of Adam. She is Adam's equal. She matches Adam in every sense, in every perspective, in every thought, and in every action. She is Adam's counterpart and his ally. She brings resources to the table, which Adam does not have. Furthermore, since Adam is perfect, it equally and logically follows his Help Meet must be the same. She is perfect. She is not some silly girl who needs a man to mold her and shape her into the woman he wants her to be. She can pull her own weight. She is grown. She thinks for herself. She is independent yet the epitome of femininity. If there were ever a goddess, she would be it. SHE IS GOD'S ANSWER TO ADAM'S INSUFFICIENCY!

Eve's significance in this Bible epic has been diluted over countless decades, so allow me to paint her for her true worth and value. Whether she is a real person or character in a story, her significance speaks volumes and I cannot allow her role to be minimized or diminished at the sake of stroking male chauvinistic theological egos. In the story, she is created from the rib of Adam. The function of the rib cage is to protect the vitals. Our lungs, heart and other organs of significance are there. The rib cage protects them. So as a Help Meet, Eve had a natural inclination to see Adam's vulnerabilities and was equipped naturally to protect him. That is strength. Something Adam could not do himself. That was a weakness. Without the rib cage, our bodies would lack adequate support to our physical frames. Therefore, Eve provided support to Adam. That was strength. Adam could not do that for himself. That was a weakness. Eve and Adam together could fulfill the mandate *"be fruitful, multiply, replenish the earth, subdue it, and have dominion over it"* but only together could they do it. Alone, they would fail. It must be duly noted as well that Eve was not there merely for the baby making purpose of the Divine Mandate. Together, they were to be fruitful. Together they were to multiply. Together, they were to replenish the earth. Together, they were to subdue it. Together, they were to have dominion over it. Again I reiterate, Eve was not inferior or subordinate to Adam. She was his EQUAL.

God made both Adam and Eve in the story. God made both with the ability to do and do well and God made both with the inability to do and not do well. I often asked myself, *"Why would God make people with weaknesses"*. It was frustrating to me. It made me angry and confused. How could preachers say God was so compassionate when it seemed to me as one big cosmic joke God wanted to play? I thought for a long time God enjoyed watching us struggle in achieving our dreams and desires. Like mice in a cage struggling, I thought God took amusement in our struggle in life. Why else would God make us with the capacity to succeed and fail at the same time when it is clearly in God's power to make us with the ability to be successful only? I contemplated the question for years until I began to see my weaknesses as something else. Eventually, I realized if we were made with all strengths and no weaknesses, we would need no one else. We would not need cheerleaders. We would not need advice. We would not need friends. We would not need counselors. We would not need people to believe in us. We would not need faith. We would not need hope. We would not need love. We would not need family. We would not need God. Truly, we would be…alone.

"It is not good that man be alone. I will make for him a help meet". Our weaknesses are invitations for help. They are opportunities in disguise to rally the support we need to reach our dreams. My grandmother was more right than I knew. Not only did God make us with weaknesses to remind us that we could not reach our dreams without God but also we cannot reach our dreams without other people as well. So we must never forget, our weaknesses are invitations for the support we need!

STOP!

BREATHE DEEP! & CONSIDER!

1. What are 2 abilities I do well?

2. What are 2 inabilities I do not do well?

3. What will turn my weaknesses into strengths?

4. How will my strengths & weaknesses affect the pursuit of my dreams?

5. Regarding my dreams, how can I maximize my strengths and position my weaknesses to become strong?

4. Faith

The final piece in assessing our inventory is our faith. *What is Faith?* **Faith** is "*the assurance and confidence in something or someone beyond ourselves*". We must discuss faith here because there is a reality we must come to grips with before we break ground to build our platform for our lives. There will be situations arising constantly in our lives. We will have responsibility and obligations to account for when those situations arise. We will take control of them. We will maneuver those situations, as we need. However, there will be other circumstances arising and they will be out of our control. We will not be able to push them as we choose. We will not be empowered to dictate what comes and what goes. We will not have the authority to make something stop or command something to begin. It will be beyond the scope of our jurisdiction. It will be outside our authority. It will be unmoved by our commands. It will be unintimidated by our position. It will simply be out of our control.

Faith is necessary at this point. It is necessary because faith gives us an assurance that surpasses the confidence we provide ourselves. Faith points us to something larger than our scope of ability. Faith directs our perspective to know something we cannot see, to believe in something we cannot command, and to be confident in something we cannot control. Faith takes us to something or someone beyond us. Whatever your spiritual or religious conviction may be, your faith will take you there. For the Hindu, some may call out to Vishnu, Shiva, or Brahma. For Christians, you may call on God or Jesus. For the Buddhist, you may look towards the Buddha. For the Muslim, it will be Allah. For the Jew, you will pray to Yahweh. For the Taoist, you will find balance in nature. Whatever our religious or spiritual conviction is, we will seek to find refuge there when events are out of our control. While we have no control over what is happening, we need to know there is something or someone who can control it. While the circumstance is uncontrollable for us, it is still controllable for someone or something else. Faith gives us a peace in knowing that. It is this peace beyond our capabilities.

Faith is pivotal to our inventory. Without it, we will waste energy and time fighting battles we cannot win on our own merit. We will wrestle valiantly but pointlessly. And when the incident does arrive where we will need to fight, we will be too tired to engage and we will lose what we could have gained. Even the atheist needs faith. Quite often we hear the word "faith" and immediately we reference something religious or spiritual. Again faith is, *"the assurance and confidence in something or someone beyond ourselves"*. We can have faith in people as well. There have been plenty of times in my life; people out the scope of my knowledge have come to my aid. This book is a testament to the example. I have written never knowing who would publish my words. It is the same in your life as well. Some of you received jobs from people you never knew. Some of you married people you met through a friend. Had they never introduced you, you would have never met. Some of you attended colleges you never thought of had someone not did a favor or made a phone call. Faith does not exclusively extend to deities but also humanity. All people are not bad. Not everyone is evil, vindictive, selfish, or manipulative. Every White person is not a racist. Every Black person is not reckless. Every man does not see you as sex object. Every woman is not out to get your money. There are good people. There are bad people. And our faith helps us have the assurance and confidence that at the time appointed, when situations are out of our control, we will be in… good hands. My friend, never lose or cast away your faith. To Breathe Deep, you will need it.

BREAKING GROUND

Now we have arrived to the part of the journey where we begin modifying our perspectives and redirecting our actions to building our platform. Everything we have discussed up to this point was designed to prepare us to grab our inner shovels and plow into the grounds of our perspectives digging new foundations full of deep breathing, clear consciousness and satisfying lives. Breaking ground is a very special moment and not one to be taken lightly. It is a single moment in time, which can never be duplicated again. It is the closing moments of one chapter and the hopeful inauguration of another. It is precious.

Breathe Deep or Die Shallow

Let us hold a ceremony right now. Let us take a moment to remember. If we are to begin a new chapter in our life today, let us stand here and remember the things, the people and the times we came through to be here. Like walking in a park, stopping, taking a deep breath smelling the flowers, let us take some time to remember where we came from. Remember your childhood. Remember the good days. Remember being carefree and worry free. Remember growing up wherever you grew up. Remember the house, the apartment, or the trailer. Remember the color of your room, your brothers, your sisters, and your imaginary friend. Remember your pet. Your hamster. Your bird. Your cat. Your dog. Remember how your pet would do little quirky things. Remember your mother and your father, your aunties and uncles, grandma and grandpa, and your cousins. Remember family vacations. Remember family dinners. Remember playing and having a good time on the streets, in the yard, and the park, or at school. Yes, remember your best friend. Remember the games you played and the songs you sang. Freeze tag. Hide & Go Seek. House. Down Down Baby up in the Roller Coaster. My mother and your mother were hanging up clothes. Remember your favorite meal as a kid. Remember your favorite Kool-aid. Let's remember our favorite cartoon show. Tom & Jerry. Popeye. Looney Toons. G.I. Joe. She-Ra. He-Man. Transformers. Robotech. Voltron. Betty Boop. Remember the church we had to go to as a kid? Easter. Christmas. Mother's Day. Remember your birthday party. Remember the color of the cake and how good it tasted. Remember your friends. Remember your 1st boyfriend. Remember your 1st girlfriend. Remember your 1st kiss. Remember your 1st day as a freshman in high school. Remember the first time you lied to your mom or dad to hang out with friends. Remember the first time you snuck out of the house. Remember going to the school dance. Remember the football games, basketball games, and the track meets. Remember the weekend parties. Remember homecoming. Remember prom. Remember Beautillion and Catillion. Remember how you felt. Remember what you had on. Remember what you were thinking. Remember your last day as a senior in high school. Remember high school graduation. Remembering promising friends you will never lose touch with them. Remember realizing some of them you will never see again. Remember making new friends. Remember losing old friends. Yes, my friend, remember.

Remember going to college. Remember going to the military. Remember getting up and going to work. Remember living at home with parents. Remember getting your own apartment. Remember how you felt. Remember your boyfriend. Remember your girlfriend. Remember how you all got together. Remember how you laughed. Remember how you all hung out. Remember you thought he was handsome. Remember you thought she was sexy. Remember feeling sick and nauseous. Remember the missed period. Remember the anxiety. Remember going to the drug store and purchasing that item. Remember being afraid to take the test. Remember being afraid to see the results. Remember the doctor visit. Remember the doctor's words. Remember telling your boyfriend. Remember telling your ex. Remember hearing your girlfriend tell you the news. Remember the phone call. Remember the fight. Remember the argument. Remember crying, balling up in the fetal position on the couch, in the bed, on the floor, or in the bathroom. Remember being angry going to the strip club, hanging with the guys, getting you some beer, drowning out your thoughts and feelings. Remember the abortion. Remember the miscarriage. Remember the day she was born. Remember how he 1st felt when the nurse or doctor placed him in your arms. Yes, remember.

Remember the rape. Remember the abuse. Remember how you felt. You remember your anger. Remember your hurt. Remember your pain. Remember the molestation. Remember how you wanted to kill yourself. Remember how you tried. Remember the nightmares. Remember the sleepless nights. Remember the helplessness. Remember how you wanted revenge, justice, and payback. Remember the break up. Remember meeting a new guy. Remember meeting a new woman. Remember dating. Remember the clubs, the restaurants, the movies, the parks, the drives, the friends, hosting parties etc. Remember meeting her family. Remember meeting his family. Remember being out and seeing your ex. Remember being on a date and see their ex. Remember when you proposed. Remember when you accepted.

Remember when you told your boys about the wedding. Remember telling your girlfriends about your engagement. Remember calling off the wedding. Remember the day you got married. Remember the church. Remember when you exchanged vows. Remember when you put the ring on her finger. Remember the look in her eyes. Remember the sound of her voice. Remember how she kissed you. Remember how she loved you. Remember your promise to each other. Remember the infidelity. Remember the counseling. Remember the fights. Remember the arguments. Remember the confusion, the rage, and the sadness. Remember the divorce. Remember the custody battles. Remember all of your bad decisions. Remember all of your mistakes. Remember doing the things you should not have done but you did them anyway. Remember the times you hurt so bad that you thought you would die. Remember you wanting to die. Remember the drugs. Remember getting high. Remember the life of sex. Remember selling yourself to make money. Remember selling her to make change. My friend, do you remember?

Many of us have come a long, long way from then to now. We have overcome so many things and what I asked about in the last couple of paragraphs does not even cover the surface for many of us. All of us may not have had everything happen to us in our memories as I asked about but all of us have had something happen to us. Life has dealt all of us some blows. Life has given all of us some sad times, depressing days, and some tragic events. We have cried. We have gotten high. We have been drunk. We have been promiscuous. We have fought, been arrested, thrown in jail, abused, molested, pimped and so much more. We have been divorced, humiliated, ostracized, mocked, taken advantage of and played for a fool. We have been beaten, shot, stabbed, thrown down stairs, choked, and poisoned. The people we loved have held guns to our heads. Knives have been held to our bodies by the ones we cared for. AND YET…WE ARE STILL HERE!

Many people would never believe our story if we told them. For many, we have tried to tell them and they could not understand. Our history is full of bitter, sweet memories. Some was our own fault. Others we had no control of what happened to us. However, today marks a new day. This day we break ground. This day we decide no longer to allow life to dictate what we feel, think or do. This day we commit to taking DEEP BREATHS. This day we commit to STOPPING and smelling the roses of life. This day we commit to CONSIDERING ourselves and contemplating who we are and why we see, think, and act certain ways. This is a monumental day. This is a day of days. This is the day we break ground and start again to live life on purpose by our rules according to our standard.

    We have discussed our foundations. We understand the significance of our context (what has happened to us). We realize the value of our perspective (our response to it). We are remembering our dreams. We have assessed our inventory. We are mindful of our strengths. We understand our weaknesses are invitations for help and support. We know our faith is a necessity. It is non-negotiable. We have remembered where we have come from and we accept it as it is. Our lives do mean more than catalogue of memories and our effort to reconcile experiences will prove it. Therefore, let us grab the shovels of our heart and raising the shovels over our head; let us make a memorial giving one huge strike into the ground of our life. To you reading this book right now, it is my privilege and honor, to present to you, the new ground on which you will build and reestablish your life. Ladies and Gentlemen, I am excited and pleased to present to you… *YOU!!!*

YOU MAY NOW TURN THIS PAGE…

BREAK GROUND & RECLAIM YOUR LIFE!!!

Chapter 1
Breaking Ground Exercise

Now it is time for you to write. I have brought all the questions I have asked you throughout this chapter back to this page. During the chapter I have asked you to stop, breathe deep, and consider. Here I ask you to stop, breathe deep, and write. Breaking ground is YOUR labor to move you to the place where you want to be. It is interactive. Engage these questions. Think about them. Answer them. If you will write, you will move yourself closer to your dreams. No short cuts to success. My friend, this is work, a work that is worth the effort and time. Invest in yourself. You deserve it. I will see you in the next chapter. NOW BREATHE DEEP & BREAK GROUND!

1. What are 2 experiences you have had and what has been your response to those experiences that now contribute to the way you see life?

2. How has your perspective of life affected your relationships and the way you communicate with other people?

3. Does your perspective make you more trusting of people or more suspicious? Why?

4. Can you see yourself developing a new response to your history? If so, how? If not, why?

5. What are 3 experiences in your life you have a difficult time accepting happened to you?

6. For each experience, what crime was committed against your heart, your body, your faith, your trust, etc. causing so much pain to make you want to deny it ever happened?

7. Was your response to each event then out of anger or out of sadness?

8. Is your perspective now bitter, hateful, skeptical, and cynical?

9. Can you see someone being enhanced by your experience if you can find the strength to share it with a hopeful insight?

10. Remember 2 of your dreams, what were they?

11. Are your dreams fulfilled, in development, or shattered? What happened?

12. What are your dreams like now or do you dream at all?

13. Can you find the courage to dream again?

14. What are 2 abilities I do well?

15. What are 2 inabilities I do not do well?

16. What will turn my weaknesses into strengths?

17. How will my strengths & weaknesses affect my pursuit of my dreams?

18. Regarding my dreams, how can I maximize my strengths and position my weaknesses to become strong?

CHAPTER 2

Thanks… but No Thank You (Discriminating Help)

"Be ye not unequally yoked together with unbelievers"
– 2nd Corinthians 6:14 KJV

When it comes to top performances from athletes, breathing is everything. While athletes possess skills, they lack physical conditioning. The lungs support the body. If the lungs lack oxygen, the body cannot perform with excellence. So the lungs and the body must be trained together in order to be an effective unit. Consequently, athletes must be placed under strenuous physical conditions constantly training their lungs to breathe and body to operate at peak performance, especially when they have not been active in the sport for an extended time (if ever). The task is always uncomfortable. Quite often, athletes are bowed over, hands on knees, trying to support themselves, panting for air as their bodies try to maximize the intake of oxygen with every inhale. Precisely at those moments, the coaches instruct athletes to stand straight. When the athlete is standing up straight more air can fill the lungs rather than when hunched over. Too much conditioning can injure an athlete and too little conditioning can ill-prepare an athlete. It is up to the coach to determine the difference. Therefore, the right coach <u>is essential for the right conditioning</u>.

    Allow me to be the first to congratulate you on beginning to reclaiming your life. Establishing your personal platform now will serve you well throughout your life and specifically through this process. Standing on your platform will empower you to have moments of breathing deep. The kind of moments where you can enjoy every action executed with maximum results, a meaningful life and a satisfying disposition. You have come a long way in just one chapter. I am sure you are excited about your progress in this process as I am. So let us continue this process as we move into drawing lines and discriminating who is and who will not be on our team.

DRAWING LINES IN THE SAND

Quite often, when people hear the scripture, *""Be ye not unequally yoked together with unbelievers"* they immediately reference dating or intimate relationship scenarios between a Christian and a non – Christian. And while those situations fit the context of the verse, it is not limited to that type of context either. We can be incompatible with people of our same faith, our same denomination, our same education, our same salary bracket, and our same ethnicity. Just because we go to the same church does not constitute we believe in the same things. Just because we make nearly the same amount of money does not mean we are safe for each other. Just because both of us have degrees does not guarantee we will think the same way on the same topics. The word *"unbeliever"* is not limited to spiritual or religious conviction alone, but in every sense of unbelief. If we are to deal with people, do business with people, make investments with people, unite our lives with people, it is imperative we believe in them and they believe in us. Without those 2 components in the equation, our efforts are futile. Without those 2 components, we are creating shallow relationships destined to produce mundane results. So there comes a time where we must draw some lines. These lines give us boundaries. They serve us like banks in a river. With these lines, we discriminate. We discriminate intentionally. We discriminate in whom we can work with and who cannot. We discriminate who can help us and who cannot. We discriminate with whom yokes up with us and who is not on the same par with us. In this chapter, we are drawing lines, making distinctions, and intentionally discriminating.

I received an email in my office one day from Ms. Glenn (a mother who wanted to get her son involved in the Boy Scouts). She left her name and number in the email and asked me to call. When I called, the phone went to voicemail. Normally, I would not have paid attention to what the voicemail said but her voicemail was quite different. It said,

> "*Thank you for calling. I am making a positive change in my life. If you are not a positive change, hang up now! If you are a positive change, leave a message and I will so kindly get back with you at my earliest convenience. Again I say I am making a positive change. Thank you. And have a nice day*".

My first reaction was, "*who in the world pissed her off*". I laughed to myself leaving my message. After I left the message, I sat there in my office thinking about her voicemail. I thought how bold she was to leave that kind of message on her phone as the greeting. Anyone could call her phone and they would hear *that* greeting. She must have been fed up with whatever she was going through or whomever she was dealing with. Whatever the case, it was apparent she wanted change and she was not intimidated by declaring her change to anyone who tried to connect with her. I met with Ms. Glenn later on that afternoon to sign her son up and I asked her about the greeting. She said,

> "*I'm tired of dealing with people who want nothing. They are down and they drag me down with them. I want more out of life than that. So I made up my mind that I wanted change. Anyone that's going to be with me MUST be a positive change. Otherwise, keep it moving*".

I was speechless and thoroughly impressed.

Ms. Glenn has done what this section is all about. She has taken her finger and drew a line in the sand. She has marked how far she is willing to go, what she is willing to deal with, and whom she is willing to deal with. She has made a dramatic declaration. And she has positioned her declaration in a highly visible and audible place where anyone and everyone will hear it. Quite often, in order to shake people out of apathy, people need dramatic examples and situations. She forced herself to execute her frame of mind by placing her decision in the full view of anyone who tries to contact her. If we are to shake ourselves out of apathy, we must position our newly established platforms in full view for other people to see. When we make our dreams public, 4 things happen. First, it empowers us to actually carry out what we said we were going to do. It's one thing to say we are going to do something and whatever it is we want to do no one knows about it but us. It is easier to never accomplish our dream or goal when no one is expecting it. It is easier to make excuses for what did not happen when the only people discussing what happened are me, myself, and I.

When I was graduating with my Bachelor's degree, I told everyone I was graduating in May. The truth of the matter was I was "*scheduled*" to graduate in May. There is a significant difference between what "*is*" happening versus what is "*scheduled*" to happen. One is certain and the other is not. While my graduation date was a real date and students would be graduating on that date, it was not a certain guarantee, I would be graduating on that day. I had 21 credits I was taking in my last semester. I had a lot of work to do and it was not getting done. I had injured myself during those last few months with a pinched Syatic Nerve in my left leg. I missed a month of classes due to laying in bed and rehab. Missing a week of college classes is like missing 2. So missing a month was like missing 2 months. However, I continued telling people I was graduating in May. People started telling me who was coming to graduation. Family started making plans to celebrate. My parents asked me what restaurant did I want to eat at on that day. My nieces and nephews started talking among themselves of what they thought it would feel like graduating from college. They started playing pretend like they were graduating. Does that concept sound familiar? Aunts and uncles started using me, as an example to my younger cousins of what hard work will do for you when you apply yourself. The heat was on. I had created an environment of expectation.

Simultaneously, my advisor was not as hopeful. He saw my progress or the lack thereof. The professors from my courses informed him on my development. It was not good. I had tests to make up, homework to turn in, quizzes to do, papers to write, and presentations to make. It was not looking good for me. I started thinking to myself,

"What am I going to tell everyone if I DON'T graduate in May". How will they react? What will they think? How will I explain this to my nieces and nephews? With the expectation of graduating as "scheduled" coming from everyone I told and with the recommendation to extend my academic stint another 6 months, I made a decision. I could not let my word be made void. I could not allow myself to speak something and I not make it come to pass. If I said I was going to do it, then I was going to do it no matter how uncomfortable it made me. I could not let my nieces and nephews down. I could not allow the expectation of me (which I created in the 1st place) be disappointed. So against academic advice from my advisor, my dean, the chaplain, and the president of the college to stay another semester, I chose to apply for graduation and execute my exit procedures. I graduated in May as "*scheduled*" with a 3.2 GPA for the same semester.

My motivation was the environment I had created. People did not expect anything from me until I started talking about it over and over again. I told people wherever I went. I sent emails. It was in my conversation. When we went out, it was part of the dialogue. I talked about graduating so much, people felt like they were the ones going to school. And when I graduated, they felt like they were the ones walking across the stage. When I struggled with studying, they pushed me on and empowered me. When I needed a break, they got me out of the house. When I started making excuses, they reminded me of my own words. I could not understand why they were so supportive. It made me nervous. I wondered what was their intention in helping me until it hit me one day. I created an atmosphere of expectation for myself. I spoke so much about graduation until people expected nothing less than graduation. The standards I set for myself were the standards people began expecting of me.

Ms. Glenn left her greeting on her voicemail for so long, people expected change in her life. They expected a positive disposition. They expected results. It is precisely this atmosphere of expectation, which drives us to live up to what we believe because we have taken our dreams public. When we breathe deep, we empower ourselves to create our own environment reinforcing us to be successful. We authorize our own context. We draw lines bringing people into our world as reinforcers, particularly in times when we stray away and lose focus.

    Secondly, when we make our dreams public, it empowers others to dream. *Do you realize we have the power to jumpstart someone else's dream?* We have the ability to empower people to own their dreams. *How do we empower people concerning their dreams?* It seems very simple but here is the answer. We must talk about our dreams. We must be consistent with our dreams. Let people hear it on our voicemails. Let them see it as a screen saver on our laptops, cell phones, and desktops. Let it be the center of our discussion. Let them see it in our bathrooms, on the mirror, in our bedrooms, and on our walls. Let them walk into our house and smell it. Let them ride in your car and hear it. Invite them to your office where they can feel it. Eventually, they will believe not only in your dreams but they will become impregnated believing once again in their own dreams as well. DREAM TALK IS CONTAGIOUS!!!

    I had spoken so much about my goals that my dreams inspired friends to dream. My goals motivated their goals. I had spoken so much about graduation until they felt they needed to graduate from something. Ms. Glenn spoke so much about change that her girlfriends started talking about the same. They had long discussions on what they were willing to deal with and what they were not. People admired her boldness and self-authorized their boldness. Never realizing it, Ms. Glenn and I (through our own life experiences) had unintentionally empowered others' dreams through our own. We personally discovered when we empower people in our lives, the success or failure of our lives directly impact them. It is as though they succeed or fail through our success and failures. We must realize our lives are connected to something far greater than our own. Our lives extend to people beyond our scope. We will impact people we will never meet. We will motivate people we will never know. We must begin to understand our lives were never our lives alone. Our lives are, will be, and have always been connected to other people.

    On the other hand, when we talk about our dreams there will

be those who criticize you and when they do, DRAW THE LINE IN THE SAND. We cannot be afraid of what they will say. We cannot allow ourselves to be intimidated by the skeptics, the cynics, or the critics. We must place our goals in front of people and allow them the opportunity to believe in it as we believe. Even if they do not believe, we must give them the chance *TO* believe. We never know where our help is coming from. It could be sitting next to us or sleeping next to us. It could be our employer or our client. It could be a friend or a stranger. We never know what resources are around us until we put it out there where we are going. We may never receive the resources we need until our dreams inspire the ones who have what we need to dream for themselves. Only when we make our dreams public, can we truly have options.

Thirdly, when we make our dreams public, we must be prepared for the fact people will make their opinions public also. Here is what we must realize, everyone will not be against our dreams but everyone will not be for them either. Some will expect great things from us. They will rally behind us and cheer. They will run to aid us where they can and constantly give us words of encouragement. These are the people we need to keep around us and on our team. Because there will be times we will run out of gas. Our self-encouragement juice will drain dry every now and again. This is when those people come in handy for us. But on the other hand, we will have the skeptics, cynics and critics to contend with as well. They will be there faithfully to critique our actions, intentions, methodologies, contacts, results, and our feelings. They will say, "*It's not possible*". We will hear them say, "*That's not practical*". And we must know there are those who will be ever so anxious to sing the song, "*I told you so*".

However, there is a reality we must take note of and carefully examine. Because someone may be a skeptic, a cynic, or a critic, it does not necessarily follow they are against us. Because they scrutinize our labor and challenge our arguments does not mean they want us to fail. I know it may be difficult to see because those types of people rub us the wrong way. It is usually this group of people who take some of what we think is our finest work and rip it to shreds limb by limb. And before we speak to them about it, we are excited. After we speak to them, we are back at the drawing board doing it all over again frustrated because we thought our effort was excellent but it feels like it was the contrary. These types of people challenge us. Usually, they are the ones who are doing what we want to do. They do not get all excited like parents and family do. Oh no my friend, these are the ones performing at the level we aspire to perform at. They write the way we want to write. They work they way we want to work. They live the way we want to live. What we must realize and accept is everyone does not see events the same way. Just as we are operating from our newly built platform, they are functioning from the same. Their perspective is much further along than ours when it concerns the craft or career we are pursuing.

An example of this is when a child writes a paper for a class giving it to his parent to read. The parent is thoroughly pleased and proud of what the child has written. The same paper receives a "C" grade. The child and the parent thought it should be an "A" paper. When the parent comes to school to raise hell to the teacher about the grade, the teacher responds, "*The paper was good in its content, but Johnny didn't cover the assignment*". Quite often as the skeptic, cynic, and critic, they are not concerned with our EFFORT only but they are looking to see if we are COVERING THE ASSIGNMENT. Their criticisms are not about us personally, but about our work. Usually we take offense to such a notion regarding our work being criticized because we see our work as an extension of us. Therefore, if our "***work***" is criticized and scrutinized, we internalize it as "***us***" being criticized and scrutinized. That is our perspective. But that is not the perspective of the skeptic, critic, or cynic. They evaluate our work and how our work will hold against other people's work in the same area. They look at our development and raise questions as to our development equipping us to be successful and sustaining success. While family and friends may look at a single event and say great job, they look at a range of events and say nice job but we need to do better. While others assess a single moment, they assess a series of moments. Therefore, the eye of the critic, the skeptic, and the cynic is as necessary for our success as the cheerleaders and fans in the bleachers.

Theses types of people are our coaches. They are the ones who know what our particular dreams, goals, and aspirations require from us. They raise questions we never thought to consider. They point out flaws we interpret as strengths. They challenge us in ways aggravating and frustrating. They stretch us. They pull us. They push us. They sign us up for events we do not think we are ready for. They send us to events we think are irrelevant. They scrutinize our efforts. They critique our ideas. They are skeptical about our methods. It seems there is no end to pleasing them until we realize pleasing them is not what they want. What they want is for us to be ready for what our dreams, aspirations and goals will throw at us. They want us ready for success when success comes knocking. They want us disciplined to sustain the success we acquire. They want us focused so we will not become intoxicated with our success. They want us to manage our careers and dreams and not the other way around. They labor to empower us to be BREATHE DEEP and not lose step. They burden us with task on top of task so we will develop time management skills not solely for our careers and dreams' sake but also how to have a personal life while still in heavy demand. They equip us with HOW to breathe deep and not lose focus. They steer us away from shallow thinking and shallow behaviors producing shallow habits accumulating into shallow existences.

We are drawing lines. We are drawing distinctions. It is necessary the skeptic, cynic, and critic have their very own section. Quite often, the skeptic, the cynic, and the critic are misunderstood. Their disposition is seen through a different lens of perspective and naturally their action follows the same. Consequently, they are labeled the "*bad guy*" because they see from a different platform and yet their critique or skepticism still has such a personal impact. Now it must be understood, not every skeptic, cynic, or critic is a coach. Not all of these types of people are in our corner either. Some are for us. Others are against us. And it is up to us to discern the assets from the liabilities and draw the lines.

STOP!

BREATHE DEEP! & *CONSIDER!*

1. Have you taken your dreams public? If so, how? If not, why?

2. Identify 3 people who are supportive of your dreams. In what way does each of them support you?

3. Identify 3 people who are skeptics, cynics, or critics. Has their opinions helped you? If so, how?

4. Identify 3 ways the supportive people differ from your skeptics, cynics, and critics in attitude and behavior.

5. Which groups do you like more spending more of your time around? Why?

Fourthly, making our dreams public positions us for attack. We must understand such an action comes with open scrutiny. Remember Ms. Glenn's positive change voicemail in the beginning of the chapter? People have criticized her for her position. People have criticized her for placing her position in her voicemail. Some have said other people do not need to know her business. Some have attacked her character. Some claim she has not changed just because she left a sassy voicemail. Whatever the scrutiny was, her motivation was not for them. She did it for herself. What those people attacking her failed to understand was, the fact that they were actually attacking her indicated the type of person she did not want to be connected with in the first place. Her attackers were the people she was cutting out of her personal life! They were the people of negativity. They were the ones she was talking about when she left the greeting on her voicemail.

This is something we must realize. As we begin talking about the new us, the revived us, the inspired us, the people we do not want to associate with will be the people who attack us. How do I identify the people who are deadly to the fulfillment of my dreams? They are the ones who tell you *"it's stupid"*, *"that doesn't make any sense"*, *"I think you shouldn't try to change"*, *"why would you do something like that"*, and *"I wouldn't read that book"*. They are the ones who freely offer criticism but never offer help. They are the ones who tell you that you are crazy for trying to do something different when they are complaining about the same problem and come to you crying hysterically when their problem is beating them up. They are the ones who misquote scriptures out of context trying to box you in the same way their preacher has boxed them in. They are the experts in everyone else's life but an amateur in their own. Those people are poison to your aspirations, sugar in your gas tank, vinegar in your Kool-aid, and manure in your wine. You ask me, *"Who do I stay away from"*. STAY AWAY FROM THEM!!!

Attacks are wonderful realities with the right perspective. They are indicators. They tell you who should be on your team. They tell you who should not. Attacks are an awesome indicator because it exposes just how much someone wants to see you fail or just how jealous they are of your success. Many times, you do not have to even be successful. Quite often, all you have to do is make up your mind you are going to take a certain action and begin moving towards it. That is enough right there for people to become jealous because you have gone further than what they did. A lot of people like to talk. They like to say what they want to do. They say what they wish for. They discuss their plans when they get to a certain place in their lives. They talk about what they are going to buy when they achieve a certain income. They say where they are going to go when they have a family. They chit chat about how romantic it will be when they get married. And yet, they never get pass talking about it! It is like they cannot register the fact that there is more to life than talking about. And for some, they spend their whole lives talking. They talk like they're paid to do it. They dispense more energy in talking about things they can change themselves (yet never do) than they do at the job that actually pays them for their work. These people I cannot stand. I cannot stand these people because they do not want change. They want us to be as miserable as they are. They want us bitter, hateful, and disgusted as they are. Misery does love company. There are so many of us reading this page right now nodding our heads up and down because we know those people I speak of. You may have just gotten off the phone with them. You may sleep with them. You may date them. You may be related to them. Whomever and wherever they are, one thing is certain, WE KNOW EXACTLY WHO THEY ARE!

Sometimes when I see them coming my way, I catch myself trying to click my heels 3 times saying, *"There's no place like home"*. We try to run in the opposite direction when we get word they are coming around the corner. We groan deep on the inside when they call us. Some of us are devout in our spiritual convictions but when they come around, our faith is severely challenged. These people are such a different breed of people and we cannot figure out for the life of us why they want to be bothered with us. We have not said anything to them. We do not call them. We do not hang out with them. We do not know their family. We do not eat at the same restaurants, shop at the same stores, get our haircut at the same barbershop, or live on the same street. And yet…they still feel the need to attack us! I can see us clinching our fists, raising them over our heads, shaking them screaming, *"LORD, DELIVER US FROM THESE CRAZY AND RIDICULOUSLY SELF DECEIVED FOLKS"*.

I personally discovered something for myself when it came to attacks. When I started practicing what I discovered I found out handling attacks became much easier to bear. One of the best ways to handle attacks is not to respond to them. It is not an infraction of your masculinity if you do not respond to an attack. Attacks are designed to get us to respond. Therefore, attacks will aim to utilize any vulnerability it can to solicit the response empowering the attack to attack us better. This is one of the reasons chapter 1 was so prevalent in helping us build our platforms. We must know where we are and where we are going. We must know our strengths and our weaknesses because attacks aim to exploit our weaknesses and manipulate our strengths. If we are not careful, we will become entangled in the web of distraction fighting fights that were never fights to begin with. We will expend energy on issues that are not issues. We will engage in arguments with no premises. In essence, we are beating up shadows. We are pounding away on the concrete with bloody hands, bruised bones, and injured ligaments attempting to make a shadow understand who we are. The problem is the shadow has no brain, no body, and has no soul. It does not have the capacity of understanding anything because it is NOT REAL! The people attacking us have arguments that are not real. Their opinions are not real. Their facts are not real. It is all a ploy to ensnare us into the place of bitterness where they are.

I mentioned earlier that attacks are indicators. We can always identify an area of great significance in our lives by the attacks it brings. So much so, that the value of our success can also be traced by the amount of an attack or group of attacks. Furthermore, we can assess the value of succeeding by the force of the attacks currently in progress. An example of pain and success is pregnancy. A woman carries a child for 9 months on average. She experiences pain and discomfort throughout the pregnancy. But the pain is at its greatest when it is time to birth the child into this world. So it is with our dreams. We can gauge the reality of our success coming to fruition by the force of attacks. Pay attention to the attacks. Do not pay attention to what the attacks are saying. Pay attention to the force of the attacks. They can be indicators of just how close you are to actually succeeding. Be mindful of your surroundings. They are always informing us.

We must draw a line in the sand. This line cannot only be for those attacking us but also for ourselves. We must set restrictions on ourselves. If we fail to do so, we will be egged into fights for no reason. And when the fight we need to fight comes, we will lose because we are too tired. We will have spent too much time fighting the wrong thing. Keep this in mind; our dreams will guide us! Remember, our dreams are always more than what we know and what we have. Our dreams are more than a destination but a standard. Our dreams keep our heads up and pushing forward. Attacks are designed to position you in a low place. People who "have" dreams are not intimidated or afraid of people who "have not". When was the last time you saw the CEO jealous of the mailroom? When was the last time LeBron James was intimidated of a 5th grade basketball player? Never. Only people who do not have get jealous. Only people afraid of losing what they have to you attack you. Bosses, managers, and supervisors, sisters, brothers, and friends, colleagues, choir members and preachers all can attack you. So if we permit ourselves to attempt answering back to any of these attacks, we take our eyes off of our dreams and face them down to the pit from where the attacks are coming from. People go where they focus their attention. If we focus our attention on our dreams, we will have our dreams. If we focus our attention on the attacks, we will become those who attack us. We will become as bitter as they are. We will become as hateful as they are because while we spent time fighting them, time did not wait for us to refocus on our dreams. And before we know it, we have become the people that spent so much time talking and never performing what we spent so much time talking about. And on their deathbed, the negative folks (who have become our coffee buddies in old age and our gossiping partners in church), say with their last dying breath, "*I TOLD YOU SO*". And only then will we realize we wasted so much time fighting them and neglecting our dreams that we became them. Only then will we realize by fighting them we made them absolutely right. They told us we could not achieve our dreams and because we used our energy to fight them, we abandoned our own aspirations. What a sad commentary to follow after the life of a person. How many people do we know who allowed other people to talk them out of their dreams? How many people are old now living with regret in hospitals, nursing homes, and homeless because someone talked them out of the life the could have had? How many people are existing right now going to jobs they really do not want, married to people they do not love, living where they do not find peace all because they fought the wrong battles and dispensed all the energy to answer unreal questions? What a tragic last note to sing, a sad last line to write, and a sad memory to have. Let us ask ourselves, "*Is that where I want to be?*" Some of us are reading this page right now because we see our lives heading in that direction. My friend, there is hope for you. The fact you are reading this demonstrates hope is ALIVE and STRONG WITHIN YOU! Join me and countless others and do as we all have done and doing even right now: DRAW A LINE

IN THE SAND and declare "*NO MORE*"!

STOP!

BREATHE DEEP! & *CONSIDER!*

1. Identify 3 people who attack you. What is the reason(s) each of them attack you?

2. How have you responded to the attacks in the past? Why?

3. Identify 2 serious attacks. What are they about?

SO YOU SAY

When we draw lines, we force people to take sides. You are either on the right side of the line or the wrong side. You cannot be on the right side and wrong side simultaneously. People must make a choice. They must vocalize their decision. When Ms. Glenn left her positive change announcement as her standard voicemail greeting, she forced people to take a side. Her announcement made 2 distinctions. First, she said, "*If you are not a positive change, hang up now*". Her 2nd distinction was, "*If you are a positive change, leave a message*". In both phrases, it was clear what she wanted. Ms. Glenn wanted a person to make a decision. She demanded a person to take a side. She wanted them to say something. Even in leaving a message, the person leaving the message was saying something loud and clear. If we are to rally the right people on our team and weed out the wrong ones, we must force people to take sides. We must compel them to SAY IT. One day a group of us were moving some friends. The girlfriend was mad at the boyfriend because he kept telling everyone what to do but was not helping us move any furniture. Finally, the girlfriend screamed at him, "**If you are going to help, then be a help. If not, then move the hell out of the way**". That attitude must be our attitude. We need people to be what they claim themselves to be. If you say it, be it! When you take a side, be what you say! We have too much work to do and too little time to do it. So if people claim they can help us, then help us. Otherwise, MOVE THE HELL OUT OF OUR WAY!

In the 1st part of her greeting, anyone who meant Ms. Glenn ill fortune was instructed to hang up. Immediately, Ms. Glenn began discriminating. Her discrimination was not based on age, gender, social status, or income. It was premised by intentions. She discriminated against the negative intentions of people. We must do the same. Usually, those are the people who assume we think we are better than them. They believe we have convinced ourselves we have arrived. They are the ones who mean us no good. They are not motivated to put in the work to get us to do what they want us to do because they know they will have to work to manipulate us. They want something easy. Ms. Glenn cut out of her life a significant number of people because she took a stand, which made it obvious *"she wasn't easy"*. No one had to guess what was her attitude. She said what was on her mind. She cornered those who wanted a one-night stand, a shallow sexual relationship, and negative individuals in the message. She called them out and instructed them not to bother her. And for every time they call the message remains the same. If we want to weed out the knuckleheads, the gold diggers, the gossipers, and the drama queens, our words must be consistent. Our message must be clear. Our point must be crystal. If you are negative, "KEEP IT MOVING".

Her 2nd distinction was, *"If you are a positive change, leave a message"*. Here is where life becomes complicated. The first section was easy. If you are a negative person, hang up. She alleviated a lot of unnecessary drama and stress from her life. Those types of people do not leave messages. They hang up. Eventually, those types of calls stop coming altogether. Howbeit though, the 2nd part of the announcement becomes much harder to sift. In the 2nd section, much more questions and concerns arise for us. It is not as simple as "positive versus negative". *Is this person "**truly**" a positive person? Is this person the "**right type**" of positive person for my goals? Can this person "**actually**" help me achieve my dreams?* It is at this juncture in our discrimination process where we encounter the liars, the manipulators, the cowards, the advocates, the coaches, the cheerleaders, the critics, the skeptics, the pretenders, the sabotagers and so much more. And ironically, they all say the same thing. *We are "**positive changes**" in your life.* However, while the truth to their declaration of disposition has yet to be proven, we have forced them to take a side and say something.

There is a reason we need people to take sides. We need a team. We cannot reach our goals by ourselves. We have weaknesses. There are things we simply cannot do and other things we are not good at. We cannot be everything. Our dreams require more than our personal know-how. They demand for more than our own experience. In order for our dreams to come to fruition, the truth is, we need help. We need a *"**Dream Team**"*. I will define a dream team as "***a specific group for specific tasks with specific abilities in achieving specific outcomes***".

These people are not recruited to our team just because they claim they can help us. They are not the regular Joe, Jack, or Jane walking the street. They are task-specific, goal-specific, and team-specific.

The 1st time I ever heard the words "Dream Team", it was in reference to the Olympics. The United States decided to enroll NBA players representing the US Olympic Team. Every major NBA star was on the team. What made the team so awesome was everyone was the best at what they did. Nobody could handle or pass the ball like Magic Johnson. No one could post up and bang it out under the boards with strength like Karl Malone and Patrick Ewing. And absolutely no one could dazzle the crowd with last second shots like Michael Jordan. The most significant thing about the team was their ability to communicate. Everyone knew who was good at what and they accepted it. They knew who to get the ball to in times of trouble. They knew who needed to handle the ball when in open court. They knew who should have the ball in the closing seconds of the 4th quarter. That is precisely what we need for our team. We need experts (or something close to it) who can help us attain the gold medals of our lives. We need people who can handle and pass the right opportunities to us like Magic. We need people we can trust to post up and bang out issues for us under strong opposition. And we need people to believe we can make the last second shots that dazzle the crowd. We need a Dream Team. And the way we select our teammates is force them to take sides and observe them to discover if they will live up to what they say.

Speaking is a very significant phenomenon. Quite often, it is difficult to appreciate speaking because we do it everyday. We hear people talk everyday. Wherever we go, someone is always saying something. Television shows, radios, meetings, work, home, church, grocery store, and wherever else, someone is always talking. Even in some of the most beautiful, serene, and quiet places, we still come across someone on the cell phone or talking really loud. If you are like me, I am sure you are thinking to yourself, "JUST SHUT UP ALREADY". I hate to sound so crass but the truth of the matter is sometimes we just want to get away from the noise of the day. We want to find a little quiet corner of the world where we can sit and hear the wind blow through the trees and onto our faces and a place where we hear the birds sing. We want to be somewhere where we hear the quiet waves of a lake. Just someplace quiet where we can take A DEEP BREATH. Yet we are constantly immersed in a life of ever-busy discussion about something. And it would behoove us to pay attention to what is being said.

When we open our mouths and speak, we are saying much more than our words only. We speak with tone and inflections. We speak with speed and diction. We can even tell what type of person we are when we talk. Even for some of us, our accents tell what part of the country or the world we are from. We can tell if you are happy or sad. We can assess if you are in love or disgusted. We can tell how you have been raised. Even our speech can indicate how accomplished we are academically. You are reading these pages and can even tell a little bit about me as the author. Yes my friend, our speech betrays us all in many ways. Yet, we still must pay attentions to the words.

We discussed earlier how taking our dreams public can create our own context. Taking our dreams public empowers us to create our own environment. We cannot take our dreams public unless we vocalize them. And it is the vocalization of others taking sides we need to hear. We need people to say where they are in regards to us. Yes, tone and diction, inflection and rate of speed are all important. But ultimately, when the rubber meets the road, we need a person to say where they are. *Why is it so important for people to vocalize their decision regarding us?* Of all the answers possible, there's one I think of. We need people to go on record. We need them to say what they have decided. This way we have a reference for them. When we think of them, we recall what they said. My grandfather taught me as a boy, "*Your word is the greatest currency you will do business with. If it loses its value, what will you negotiate with*"? We need to appraise the value what people say to us. Forcing people to take a side is one thing. Appraising the value of what they said is another. *How do we appraise the value of what people say to us?* By their actions and the consistency of their words. We can measure the value of others words by what actions follow after what they say. Do they do as they say they will? Do they show up when they say they will? If they say they love you, when was the last time they put you before themselves? If they say they will listen to you, when was the last time you were allowed to ramble without interruption? If you are so special, why have they not made time for you? If my grandfather was correct in what he told me, many people we know are negotiating contracts with WORTHLESS CURRENCY! They do not keep to what they say. And what is worse than what was just mentioned; people who do not keep their word when no one is watching them.

In the creation story, I often wondered why did God say everything was good when God made it. It baffled me to no end. *Was it good just because God said it was good?* The concept seemed quite shallow to me and the equivalent of "*do what I say do because I'm your parent*". Yes, I hated that argument too as a kid. I went to a couple of preachers and they gave me some of their theological insight. One said, "*God didn't say it was good. Someone wrote [that] God said it was good but God didn't say it was good*". I thought to myself, "*whether or not God truly said it was good, no one knows because no one was there; nonetheless, it's in the book, man. So you got to explain it*". I was quite frustrated with him and decided at that moment I would not be going to his church. I asked another and he said, "*God is law. Therefore, his word is law. And what God says is good is good because God is law*". I thought to myself, "*It's philosophical but it's still the same "it's good because I say so" argument.* I needed more. I wrestled with it until I thought about my grandfather. Poppa was always doing what he was supposed to do even when it seemed no one was really watching. Hence, why I liked sneaking up on him and watching him work. I tried to catch Poppa slipping up like he would always catch me. I wanted to have one of those "aha" moments. It never happened. I remember him talking about **integrity**. He defined it as, "**doing what you're suppose to do when no one is watching**". I thought to myself God is integrity. God does what God is supposed to do when no one is watching God. The only person around when God created everything was God. Therefore, what made everything God made good was because God did exactly as God said God would do, even when no one was watching God. God was alone. And God still kept God's Word when no one was there to see God do something different. Hence, why we value so much of what God says about us because God performs what God says even when no one is watching. That concept truly is *"good"*. We need people who will keep their word even when no one is watching them. For those who keep their word, mark that person. We want them on our team. For the one who does not, mark them. They will not be getting a team uniform. We need men and women of integrity around us!

We have forced people to take a side. We have their "word" on record. We know how to appraise the value of their word. Now we have to beware of the one who straddles the line. Watch out for the man who changes his mind over and over again. Beware of the woman who is on your side today and against you tomorrow. Those who straddle the fence, we call *"double agents"*. Double agents are selfish people. Their only concern is their well-being. They will be on your side as long as it serves their purpose. When it no longer serves their purpose, they take your secrets and sell them to the highest bidder. They pimp out your dreams. They prostitute your gifts. They exploit your aspirations. These people only care for themselves. If they join your team and push you to do what is best for them, you have yourself a double agent. If people know more about your business than your own team does, you have a double agent. If your secrets are aired out like public service announcements, then you have a double agents. They will stay on your team until you identify them and kick them out of your life or until they have no further use for you. They are "shady". They speak out of both sides of their mouth. They are almost like dual personalities. We need stability in our lives. We do not have time to live episodes of a movie. We do not need the drama. If you have a double agent in your life, find them, and dismiss them. Their word is no good. Their company is not welcomed. And we do not need their advice. DISMISS THEM AND BE DONE WITH THEM.

STOP!

BREATHE DEEP! & *CONSIDER!*

1. Identify 3 people you told your dreams to. What commitments did each of them make to you?

2. Thinking of the same 3 people, how have they fulfilled their commitments to you?

3. Are you satisfied with their effort to perform what each of them promised to you? Why or why not?

4. Who are the "double agents" in your life?

5. Who would you like on your "dream team"? What areas of expertise do you think they will contribute to?

<u>YES YOU & NO YOU</u>

Here we come to decision time. Decision times are moments of realization for all of us. At these junctures, we choose who we want to help us and whom we don't. Some people we'll say "*yes*" to and to others we'll say "*no*". We will always be developing our team. There will be people who we had on our team that once upon a time worked with us and now work against us. There will be others not on our team who have changed their perspectives, habits, and lifestyles that we now can use as viable assets. We will always be saying "*yes*" to someone and "*no*" to someone else.

In these moments we realize we can achieve certain tasks with certain people in our lives and moments of recognizing some relationships are simply no good for us. This is a difficult time. Life is all about relationships. We live our entire lives to make the right relationships, which in turn gives our life meaning, significance, and connection. We live for these special bonds that define us, encourage us, and carry us through experiences seemingly rendering us powerless.

And yet, when decision times are upon us, there will be some relationships we will sadly have to end. Please do not underestimate or minimize such an important time. So many of us never reach our dreams because we cannot make the decision between choosing what's best for us or choosing what's best for other people at our own dream's expense.

Now hear me clearly on this matter. I am not saying there are not moments where we may choose to place our dreams on hold to preserve or develop significant relationships. Many of us who have careers and families have faced decisions compelling us to forego career advancement and promotion for the sake of preserving marriages, families, and significant intimate relationships. I know have. In other cases, people have chosen careers over developing a family with the hope that a family will be developed in the future. In some cases, they did establish a family. In other cases, they remained single looking for alternatives. **The outcomes of our life are never guaranteed no matter how well we plan them.** This is a reality we all must remember especially those of us who live and die by planning. All we can do is plan the best way we know how, be mindful of our intentions, utilize our resources, manage whatever we can manage within our ability to manage them, execute our plans, and have faith that whatever we cannot control, God can.

There is so much on the line when it comes to decisions like these. It is more than keeping a boyfriend or girlfriend. It's more than stroking people's ego because you chose to stay rather than go. These decisions mean more than choosing the promotion with the 15% bump in salary and relocation rather than the 5% increase at the same position in the same location. OUR LIFE IS ON THE LINE! What our life will look like 5, 10, 15 years from now will dramatically be impacted by the decisions at our feet NOW! We do not have the luxury of putting the decision off until tomorrow. If we do, the same choice must be made with less time to spare. For many of us, we are at our fork in the road. Do we choose the career making 6 figures and run the risk of losing a relationship we have come to cherish? Do we stay choosing another path so we can be with that special someone at the risk of secretly despising his/her existence or hating ourselves if the relationship fails later on down the line? Do we choose to walk this course and risk being indefinitely alone or do we settle for what's safe and familiar?

 I dare not to think myself more highly and qualified to advise you on what to do. I have found myself in the situation quite often and choosing the right thing to do is never an easy choice. We all want to be happy. We all want to have peace and serenity. We all want to be with someone who loves us. And we all want to have careers that bring us more joy than sorrow. However, quite frequently those notions are pitted against each other and times arise where we must choose either or. Permit me to confess to you. I have made bad decisions. I am not the author divorced from mistakes and immune to errors. On the contrary, I am well acquainted with bad decisions. I have lost friends and allies by my own carelessness. I have ostracized myself due to my own choices. And some have gone so far to ask me, "*Do I regret anything*" and my answer is, "*No*". From time to time, I miss my friends and allies that my bad decisions pushed away. I would be a liar if I told you otherwise. Nonetheless, I don't regret what I did though I miss them. I know it may sound contradictory, so allow me to explain. As I look back at my life, I know why I made the decision. At the time I thought it was best choice to make (regardless if it was selfish in retrospect). I was as informed of my decision at the time I made my choice as I could allow myself to be. It would not and did not matter about any other voice of reason because I was not in the frame of mind to hear it. I knew what I wanted and I went after it and the consequences followed. I am the man that I am now because of those bad decisions and learning from them. You are the man and woman now because of the choices (good, bad, and indifferent) you have made and what you learned from them.

 Now, of course we could spend our time wondering what if we had done something different, where would our lives be now, but why? Why waste our time with useless speculation about experiences we can never change. Why mull over bad choices when, if we allow ourselves to look a little further, we can see the good that followed? I am not saying we should not learn from our past, but I am saying we should not dwell on it. Why waste time crying over spilled milk, while the milk you have is getting sour? WE ARE TOO EASILY DISTRACTED BY OUR PAST AT THE EXPENSE OF OUR PRESENT. End the vicious cycle. Live in your present. Plan for your future. Learn from your past.

We must make choices. There are no 2 ways about it. As my father would say there are no "if's", "and's" or "but's" about it. We must make choices. There it is plain and simple, cut and dry. The reality is there are people worth placing our dreams on hold for in order to cultivate the relationship. THIS DOES NOT MEAN YOU ARE FORFEITING YOUR DREAMS! It just means there is a "temporary delay" to get the right people in the right places. We are responsible for constructing and managing our team. Life can be hard by itself. We don't need extra people making life difficult. Then there are those people who we must separate ourselves from. This does not mean they are bad (though it doesn't mean they are not either). What it does mean is that where we are going with our lives, they are more of a hindrance than an asset. These decisions have nothing to do with them being nice, sweet, compassionate, supportive, or friendly. It has everything to do with what our dreams are demanding of us and the people who will help us get there. Some of the successes I have experienced in my life required people to hurt my feelings and be aggressive with it. I needed that. Be mindful of the demands your dreams are making of you and the people you enlist to help you. A team of all nice, sweet, friendly people can be just as detrimental as a team of arrogant, pompous, educated experts. **Listen to the demands of your dreams.** I am not here to tell you whom you should say "yes" or "no" to. That choice is yours alone. I am here to remind you whomever you choose, make sure they have your best interests at heart. Do what is in your hands to do and do it well, and with everything else, let the chips fall where they may.

Live life and enjoy the ride. Why else live? Who knows what's down the road and around the corner? Who knows what tomorrow will bring? Don't you want to find out? I know I do.

YOU MAY NOW TURN THIS PAGE…

AND DRAW LINES IN THE SAND!!!

Chapter 2
Lines in the Sand

We have talked about various ways to identify help. And like chapter 1, I have collected all of the questions in this chapter so you can answer them and begin drawing lines in the sand. Take your time. You are taking a personal position in your life and this position will revolutionize everything you do from here forward. This race is not given to the fastest reader or the strongest writer. This race is given to the one who crosses the finish line with the necessary tools to help you live your life with a little more meaning and significance. SO TAKE A DEEP BREATH, AUTHORIZE YOURSELF & WRITE.

1. Have you taken your dreams public? If so, how? If not, why?

2. Identify 3 people who are supportive of your dreams. In what way does each of them support you?

3. Identify 3 people who are skeptics, cynics, or critics. Has their opinions helped you? If so, how?

4. Identify 3 ways the supportive people differ from your skeptics, cynics, and critics in attitude and behavior.

5. Which groups do you like more spending more of your time around? Why?

6. Identify 3 people who attack you. What is the reason(s) each of them attack you?

7. How have you responded to the attacks in the past? Why?

8. Identify 2 serious attacks. What are they about?

9. Identify 3 people you told your dreams to. What commitments did each of them make to you?

10. Thinking of the same 3 people, how have they fulfilled their commitments to you?

11. Are you satisfied with their effort to perform what each of them promised to you? Why or why not?

12. Who are the "double agents" in your life?

13. Who would you like on your "dream team"? What areas of expertise do you think they will contribute to?

CHAPTER 3

Here We Go Again (Coping with Frustrating Conversations)

"Can two walk together, except they agree"
– Amos 3:3 (King James Version)

Breathing is not always as easy as we would like to think. There are times we are going somewhere and our breathing is forced to change (running, climbing, altitude changes). A conflict occurs. Our normal habit of breathing wants to remain constant against a situation demanding for breathing differently. If changes are not made, we could collapse, pass out, and potentially hurt others and ourselves. So what do we do?

Congratulations! You are in the 3rd chapter of this book! How does it feel? I'm sure you have dealt with some of the challenges we have discussed in chapters 1 and 2. I'm sure you have dealt with people looking at you crazy, the whispering gossipers who pretend to be your friends, and the obvious negativity from haters. Moreover, I'm also confident you have seen yourself in a new light, experienced people who support and even have taken ownership to help you achieve your dreams. It is a beautiful thing to see your life become YOUR LIFE! I never said this would be an easy journey, but it is a journey so worth having. I am learning so much as I take on the honor and privilege to invest into you the little lessons I've learned and am still learning. I hope you are learning more about yourself, valuing who you really are, and seeing the beauty of your life for all that it is, for all that it isn't, and for all that it shall become.

WHO AM I TALKING TO

We can never get away from talking to people. We can't get away from communicating ideas, feelings, desires and more to others. From personal dispositions to business proposals, we will forever have to talk to someone. And it is usually in having those conversations where our frustrations become apparent. We talk. They talk. We talk more. They talk more. We feel our points ignored. They feel their points minimized. We become angry and they become aggravated. And what was intended to be a beneficial sharing of ideas and thoughts ends up a frustrating experience where we want to say nothing more to them and we want them to say nothing more to us.

However, while we must talk to people, very rarely do we take the time to ask ourselves whom these people truly are? We know their names. We know what they like to do. We know whom they dated but we do not know them. Most of us define who other people are by what they do. Hence, this is why men tend to be workaholics more than women (though there are a growing number of women in this category). In America, the worth of a man is qualified by his ability to produce a livelihood for him and others. The more of a livelihood a man can produce, the more of a man he is in the eyes of other men and women. And while it is important men should produce for their families and themselves, our masculinity must be more than our profession. Otherwise, we (as men) become only as valuable as the numerical value on a paycheck.

In the same breath, women are not dismissed from the misdiagnosing practice either. If it is true that men are considered real men by what they do, then women are considered real women by what they have. Socially speaking, there are circles that say that women with long hair are preferred before women with short hair. Slim women are preferred before healthier women. For African American women, lighter complexions are preferred before darker. The more clothes you have, the more shoe variety you possess, the nicer your makeup looks, and the more men crave, lust and pant after you, the more of a woman you truly are. So many women have become jealous of what other women have and are completely clueless to whom these women truly are.

So why do we experience frustrating conversations? I submit one of the main reasons we experience it is because we don't know the person we are talking to. We think we know them because we sleep with them, or take them out to eat, or laugh with them, or go to the movies with them. However, those are just activities and events we do with them but sharing those moments don't constitute knowing the person. And while we hope to discover who they truly are, the process of knowing someone is more of a process than making memories with them. WE MUST ENGAGE THEM! Why does he say he believes in God but won't go to church? Is it because he's playing the God card to get you to have sex with him? Has something happened in his past that causes him pain when he thinks of "church"? Is he a preacher who has stepped away from the limelight to discover God in a way that is beyond the pulpit, the title, and the biblical hypocritical rhetoric? Why does she not like to talk about her past? Is she just being dramatic to solicit your attention? Is she in a witness protection program? Is she ashamed of a secret? Is she running from something?

Knowing people is tough and challenging. We have layers. We have degrees of access. We have points of no turning back. We have trust issues. We all have been hurt, violated and disappointed at some point in our lives. All of us have dealt with them the best way we knew how at the time the experienced happened. We even fight others depending on how close they come to the line we have quietly drawn within ourselves. But the reality is, all of us still want to be understood. All of us want someone to hear us, feel us, relate to us, and bond with us. We crave it. We long for it. We lust after it so much we go from bed to bed or relationship to relationship seeking human interaction that is fulfilling. We look for that person who can touch us and know who we truly are. Often times, preachers tell us that only God can fulfill our needs but they aren't the ones going home alone. People say all you need is Jesus but Jesus hasn't come to your house and sat down and talk to you when you felt your world was falling apart. I am not advocating the irrelevancy or disrespecting of God, Jesus or any other religious deity. What I am saying is the reality of a practical human touch is priceless. Being a Christian or any other religion does not dismiss the basic human need for practical interaction. And at our core, just like we know God understands us, we desire so much that others understand us as well.

So we come to face to face with a question. Who am I talking to? You are more than your profession, more than your paycheck, more than your hair, more than your figure and more than your weight. We ask ourselves the question. Who am I talking to? It is a question worth taking several moments to ponder. It is an inquiry deserving the respect we have to give because people's lives and the experiences that make people who they are should never be taken for granted or lightly. Who am I talking to? This question initiates a process worth having and that process is a challenging process because that process requires us to first engage ourselves. Once again, as we face others, we face ourselves. As we talk to others, we evaluate ourselves. People stretch us. They cause us to take steps in areas we didn't plan to go. They pull us in directions we didn't map out. And when we take on the task of learning who people really are, we take on responsibility of safeguarding what is revealed to us. To deal with people is to deal with success and mess. Life is a messy affair. Therefore, to deal with people, we must understand we will deal with messy situations as well. There it is plain and simple. TO DEAL WITH PEOPLE IS TO DEAL WITH MESS!

So forewarning to you my dear friend, before you try to discover who you are talking to, ask yourself the question, "***Am I ready to hear and be responsible for what this person will disclose to me***"? If you can answer, "yes" with genuine honesty and integrity to yourself, then proceed on. If not, then don't ask the question, "Who am I talking to", because you are not ready for the responsibility that comes with having someone share the stories of their past. And there is nothing wrong with not being ready to hear someone's secrets. That is a compliment to you. It is an indicator you have matured within yourself to know what you are and are not ready for. Your perspective about yourself is bringing you closer to the tangible reality of your dreams.

My marketer asked me, "Why is knowing someone so important to living a life of breathing deep?" I told her because we need people to get to where we are going. There is not a single human being who has all the answers and the means of executing them. Geniuses need sponsors. Presidents need cabinet members. Kings need advisors. There is no one exempt from help. Jesus needed Simon's help to carry his cross. Muhammad needed Kadijah. Martin needed Coretta. Gandhi needed his family. No one is exempt from help. Therefore, we must take time to learn, discover, and truly see those who have taken up our banner and champion our causes. If we fail to know those who celebrate us, whom shall we truly know indeed?

STOP!

BREATHE DEEP! & *CONSIDER!*

1. Have I asked people about who they truly are without asking myself was I ready to be responsible for what I heard?

2. What was my response?

3. What was their response?

4. Have many of my conflicts with others happened because of me misdiagnosing who I thought the person was compared to who they truly were?

5. Do I believe there is a value in discovering who people truly are? Why or why not? _____

Understanding people is essential to the success of our dreams. We need people. I cannot reiterate enough the significance of others.

We need what they know. We need what they have. We need their connections. Therefore, it becomes a relational issue that we do not allow ourselves to treat people as a means to an end but to always treat people as people, regardless of their connections, resources, or know-how. Taking time to know people helps us to avoid exploiting them. While most of us would never intentionally exploit a person, all of us have the potential to exploit someone if we become consumed by our own agendas and goals. Investing our time with people, learning what experiences make them who they are, discovering their motivations, are all ways to safe guard the integrity of our relationship and become accountable to the people helping us. **One of the saddest tragedies occurring in our relationships is we don't trust people enough to become accountable to them**. We trust their money. We trust their connections. We just don't trust them. We have silently and passively stated, "I WILL TRUST YOUR RESOURCES MORE THAN YOU". In order for our dreams to have lasting success, we must move beyond cultivating the benefits of a relationship to cultivating the relationship itself. We must return back to valuing people. People have always been the true currency for success in life. How we live life will be based on how we treat people. Business success is based on how many people consume a product. Church services would be nothing if no one showed up. IF YOU ARE TO BREATHE DEEP IN LIFE, YOU MUST VALUE PEOPLE.

Let's look at some ways to help us redirect our attention to people and away from focusing on their wealth.

- Be Up Front

    People appreciate honesty. We like it when people don't try to pull our strings with flattery, gifts, and excessive compliments. We like it when people can get to the bottom line at the onset. Now, I'm not saying flattery, gifts, and compliments are bad. I am saying let those items enhance what you have to say and not be the basis of what you have to say. Wasting people's time is a sure way to lose allies.

When I moved to Cleveland and met with the VP of Human Resources for United Way, he told me, "Say it out front, so it won't stick out from the back". Let people know why you are there. And be there because you want their friendship, not only their wealth.

- Take An Interest In Their Projects

    All of us like it when people want to talk about us. Even those of us who are humble or claim to be humble still enjoy people taking an interest in us. So inquire about the projects they are involved in. You may discover some of the things they are doing are things you want to do. You may discover both of you have the same passions and without pitching your cause, you may already have a friend.

- Listen

    You would be surprised how much people don't listen. OK, allow me to be frank, you would be surprised how much WE don't listen. I use to think I was a great listener until my significant other pointed out I sucked at hearing what she had to say. And she was absolutely correct; I was horrible at listening to her. I talked and listened to her based off of what I thought was important and not listening to her. So listen to people. If you ask a question, be quiet and let them answer.

- Share With Them Who You Are

    This can be a challenge for some of us. There are some of us that find it easier to talk about others and find it difficult to talk about ourselves. However, people like to know whom they are dealing with.

So tell them. Tell them your dreams. Tell them your history. Tell them where you are. Tell them about your family. I have found out people are more likely to open up to you when you open up to them first. We are not playing poker. We are building relationships. So have a pleasant face, be cordial, and share. Always remember, everyone loves a smile.

Much of our frustrating conversations and the cycle thereof occur because of our lack of developing real relationships. We have focused on the benefits and negated the person. Let's change our perspective. Let's see people, value people, and talk to people for who they are. This way, their resources are not a focus but a benefit from the relationship. And that's exactly what their resources should be – benefits, nothing more!

NAVIGATING INTIMATE CONFLICT

Intimacy is something we crave. There is no gender difference to this. Race, financial stability, career advancement and social status weigh nothing when compared to this single reality; all of us long to be close to someone. It is part of our nature. We desire to bond with someone in ways not shared with others. We want to be touched, held, kissed, and made love to. And we want all of that from someone special. We want to know we can go home to someone who will be there waiting for us. We desire to have that emotional support that can't be duplicated by merely having someone share our bed. And most of us (though we would never stand on the mountain top and admit this) are quietly screaming at the top of our voices for it while having pleasant smiles, delightful voices, pressed suits, and successful careers. We are the envy of the company and go home everyday to an empty house. We are financially sound and cannot find anyone to make us laugh or watch a movie with. People know our accomplishments and no one seems interested in us. We go to church and hug countless people and no one ever touches us. Yes, there are plenty of us, surrounded by people and yet, so alone. People talk to us and no one is listening. People are jealous of us and have no clue as to what we feel. Yes, if anyone longs and craves for intimacy – WE DO!!!

And when we finally get someone who gives it to us, it is like the weight of the world has been lifted off our shoulders. Finally, we can share our souls with them. We can give them our heart. We can put our fists down and stop fighting. We can let down our guard and truly be ourselves. We can give them our body and know we won't be exploited. We can talk about things that matter to us and we can hear about what matters to them. We can exchange our ashes for beauty. We can trade in our sorrow for joy. Yes, finally, we can be connected. Finally, we have that bond with someone and there is no language uttered on the face of this planet or any other that can articulate with crystal clarity the feeling of being intimate with that one soul.

But now, we have a problem.

Now, our lives are moving somewhere beyond where we currently are. We want more for ourselves. We desire to see our dreams come to fruition. Our goals are coming alive. We can taste success in a new way. It's in the air. We feel it. The climate of our life is changing. Our winter experiences are transitioning into spring blessings. What we thought would never happen is unfolding before our very eyes. It's amazing. It's wonderful. And yet we are still so frustrated. Our frustration is not in the transition moments of our life but it's in the failure of the one we love moving with us. We are in a very exciting moment in our lives, the personal dreams we have are within reach, yet we are aggravated by the fact that we can't enjoy them because we are constantly wrestling with a love that fights us more than supports us. Our success becomes minimized in the light of our relational frustration. We can't jump up and down at the promotion we have just received because our spouse never wanted us to have the job in the first place. We can't go to the gala and smile and receive the accolades of success from our counterparts, when our significant other doesn't believe in our cause. And we are frustrated, saddened, and yes even angered about such a complex dilemma. We have no clue what to do. We don't know who to talk to. And for those of us who do have someone to talk to, their advice doesn't really give us an answer to our situation. We can't talk to our significant other because we have talked about it over and over again and in most cases, it ends up an argument or worse. We can't just walk away because we love them. We have invested our life into them. Our heart and soul are in their hands and though this situation is not a situation we want, in our hearts we don't believe the complexity of this warrants us to abandon what we worked so hard on. Nonetheless, the question remains – WHAT DO WE DO?

STOP!

BREATHE DEEP! & *CONSIDER!*

1. What are you "feeling" right now?

2. What are you thinking of right now?

Yes, my friend, it is precisely here where the reality of our dilemma becomes clear to us. There are no easy answers. And it feels, at this point, we will lose something no matter what we choose. And whatever the "something" is, it's precious to us and we don't want to lose it. If we yield to appease our significant other or spouse, we forfeit our dreams. If we press on pursuing our dreams, we're afraid we'll lose our loved one, our spouse and perhaps our family. And for some of us, that's exactly what's happening right now. Losing a husband or a wife is bad enough but your spouse is not just making it about you and him/her, but they are throwing the family on the table as well, looking us square in the face and saying – CHOOSE! All we can do is stand with tears in our eyes, stand in amazement, sit in confusion, sit enraged and ask ourselves, "*How did we get here?*" We say over and over in our mind, *"It's not fair"* or *"I would support him or her without an ultimatum"*. We ask, *"How can they be so selfish"*, *"Why can't they see this is important to me"*, or *"Why do I have to make a choice?"* It seems no matter what question we ask others, or ourselves we can't figure out why we arrived here. All we know is that we're here and it makes us feel angry, powerless, helpless, frustrated and saddened. All we know is **THIS MESS AIN'T FAIR!!!**

I can relate to the feelings you are having. Being a divorced man myself, I understand the fears of not wanting to lose your marriage or a significant relationship and I know maneuvering the pain of a broken heart, a shattered relationship, and a failed marriage. I'm familiar with asking myself what to do. And as I said before, there are no easy answers. However, there are 4 navigational steps we can discuss which may help us overcome coping with frustrating conversations and complex intimate dilemmas.

- **Do You Want To Be With Me?**

    It seems like a very simple question but make no mistake, it is quite loaded. When I contemplated breaking up with my girlfriend, it was a difficult decision to make. We couldn't talk about certain topics without it becoming an argument or a debate. I hated the fact that I loved this woman with my entire being and we couldn't see eye to eye. I had done things that hurt her and vice versa. But things really started becoming serious when I realized that my life was taking a change. I knew I had to make a decision and soon. I couldn't afford to waste time because she was looking at residencies throughout the nation after she graduated from Med School and I could not just remain silent. I decided to call her and setup a meeting for us to come to one decision. DO YOU OR DO YOU NOT WANT TO BE WITH ME? That's what it boiled down to for me. I called both of my mentors and my father for their advice. They all pointed me back to myself and advised me to ask what did I want. So I wrote 4 pages of questions to ask her. It was more of an interrogation. And the results of that were sure to push us to end our relationship because the situation was already tense and all I would have done was aggravated it more. My director saw something was bothering me in a meeting because I was extremely short and after the meeting pulled me off to the side. I told him what was up and he said, "*Phillip, all you need to do is ask her does she want to be with you. No 21 questions. Just a simple yes or no will do. Everything else is secondary. If she says yes, then both of you have a platform to build your relationship but without that, you have nothing*". I thought it was too simple for such a complex problem. Yet after 3 hours of arguing, crying, talking, venting, and the more, she said she wanted to be with me and I told her the same.

As James told me, so I reiterate to you. Do you want to be with them and do they want to be with you? No 21 questions. A simple yes or no will suffice. If they say yes, you have a foundation to work with (assuming you want to be with them). If they say no, you know where your relationship stands. But without an answer, you truly have nothing. Moreover, you must ask yourself the same. If you want to be with them, then half the battle is won because you know where you stand. If you don't want to be with them, then don't lie to yourself. Be honest and say what you don't want. I didn't say it would be easy. Yes, you will have to deal with the emotions of the moment. Yes, you will have to explain yourself and question yourself afterwards. Yes, you will still have to deal with the phone calls, the emails, and perhaps the letters. Yes, you may even still have to see them. **One of the most difficult lessons I had to learn is we owe it to people and ourselves to tell the truth, even when we know it hurts them, more than it hurts us.** I know the rationale may seem screwed. However, I have seen so many people sacrifice the truth of the situation to appease someone else's feelings and the result was catastrophic. I've been in relationships where I remained silent and quietly held in contempt in my heart for the woman. I know women who sleep with their significant other daily and silently despise them. Silence can be more deadly than speaking the truth. Imagine your special "boo" or spouse having an STD and never telling you. Imagine getting pregnant for your husband so he can have a son or a daughter and he never told you he had children already. Imagine your loved one taking a job in the city so they can be closer to you and you never told them that you were seeing someone else. Often times, truth is hard. Yet in all cases, truth is necessary. For if we cannot stand for truth, what can we stand for? What else is there to stand for?

Now allow me to be clear on the matter I just spoke of. I am no master at the telling the truth. I would love to be, but the reality is I'm not. It would be remiss of me to portray the image of being one who speaks the truth without conscience. However, just like you, I have lied. I have withheld telling my feelings and experienced the consequences. The decision to tell the truth is never easy. I've heard it said people would prefer a good lie than a bad truth. As unfortunate as that may sound, I've found it to be correct.

Remember, it's not a crime to be true to you. It's a tragedy when you are not. SO MAKE A DECISION. Indecisiveness will kill opportunities. To be indecisive about what color to paint our house, what meal to order, or what shoes to purchase compares to nothing when decisions we make directly impact someone else's life. We cannot tip toe around that matter. If we want to be with them, then be with them. If we don't, then let them know so they can go on with their lives. But to fail in making a decision, is SELFISH.

- **Drama is Temporary**

Getting an answer to whether or not the two of you want to be with each other is only the beginning. This answer doesn't mean the drama will change overnight. It does mean both of you mean more to each other than the current drama and that is something we so easily lose sight of. ***We forget problems are not eternal but temporary***. We become so consumed by current predicaments we cannot see past the present. We act as if the argument will last forever. We behave as if we will perpetually disagree. If we aren't careful, we will sabotage our own precious love. When an argument happens, we must remind ourselves, it's just an argument. We are not negotiating matters of national security or public policy (and if you are you shouldn't – leave work at work). We aren't redefining molecules of the cosmos. We are having an argument – 2 opposing views colliding on one given topic. Did you hear me? The argument is over a TOPIC not the RELATIONSHIP. Don't start fires that have no reason to exist. Though the problem may be happening in the relationship it doesn't mean the relationship is problematic. Keep the conflict in PERSPECTIVE, my friend.

Moreover, the argument should not be all over the world. It's not your opportunity to snowball or compound problem after problem. That's a sure way to aggravate your already tense relationship. If you think he is inconsiderate of you sexually, then let that be your point. Don't use his snoring during sleep as your argument. The man is sleep. He can't help it. Express what you really feel. If you think she is too absorbed in her career, don't criticize the new shoes she bought. That's not what you really want to say. Be honest with her and yourself. Only with honesty and compassion, can real problems have a real chance at real solutions.

We clash with people for many different reasons. Our loved ones are not exempt from it. In all actuality, the conflict will occur more because we are intimate with them. They know us and we know them. We have each other's secrets. We see each other in ways others don't. We spend more time with them than anyone else. Of course, we're going to get on each other's nerves. Of course, we're going to say things aggravating the hell out of one another (sometimes on purpose). Yes, my friend, conflict in an intimate relationship is inevitable. It's not the end of the world. It's just a conflict. So deal with the conflict and move on.

Now for those of us wrestling with habitual conflicts, those are temporary too. Obviously, there is something going unaddressed contributing to why the problem remains a problem. Perhaps, the problem is not others, but ourselves. Perhaps we aren't as honest with ourselves as we would like to think. Perhaps, we lack the courage to do what is necessary. Perhaps, the problem really isn't a problem but we make it a problem because of our ego and pride. In whatever scenario, the problem won't last forever. We must do our part to alleviate pressures we control and allow our faith to alleviate pressures we can't. This too shall pass, my friend.

- **Be Faithful To Your Dreams**

Not only must we stand for truth but also we must be faithful to our dreams. Why do you think you are experiencing turbulent times right now in the first place? It's not because of your new cars, your career advancements, your new house, your wardrobe, or your overall success. It's because you have chosen to be faithful to your dreams. We have followed the rhythm of our souls. We are marching to the beat of our destinies. So the worst thing you or I could do is abandon the very thing giving us hope and placing us in the lion's den in the first place. Just think, if we abandon our dreams now because of the pressures all around us, then it was all in vain to begin with. Especially when it comes to our intimate relationships, we wrestle with postponing our dreams to appease the other. Here's my 2 cents; DON'T DO IT! *Relational compromise and self-sabotage are 2 extremes on the same continuum and the line separating them is very thin.* If we start denying our dreams now to appease the other, we will never reach our goals. Furthermore, we will sentence ourselves to a relationship of quiet contempt due to how we managed the dilemma we are wrestling with right now.

- **Keep Talking**

Ok, let's call a spade a spade. When we argue and

fight with our spouses and significant others, the last thing we want to do is keep talking. Nonetheless, if we are to overcome frustrating conversations, we must keep talking. The concept of "keep talking" doesn't translate into "over-talking". I define "keep talking" as – continually creating opportunities for you and your significant other to invest in each other. This is easy to do when 2 people meet each other. We go out to movies, eat dinner, talk on the phone, send text messages, and socialize with friends and family. As a result, we learn so much about each other avoiding potential misunderstandings because we continually engage one another. But when frustrations occur in our relationship, many of us tend to disengage. Rather than investing, we divest. None of us like conflict. None of us like arguments. Even if we are right in what we say, arguments are simply emotionally taxing interactions. If you're like me, I'd prefer to stop talking than to argue. However, arguments happen and the last thing any of us want to do is self-sabotage our relationship by starving it and divorcing ourselves emotionally. While we may silence the argument by not communicating, we open up our relationship for many more problems.

These are just a few navigational concepts to keep in mind when attempting to maneuver through intimate conflicts and difficult relationships.

STOP!

BREATHE DEEP! & CONSIDER!

1. What past or recent experiences make me crave being close to someone?

2. Do I spend more time fighting in my relationship than receiving support?

3. Which of the navigational concepts do I most relate to? Why?

4. Do I hold a quiet grudge against my significant other or spouse? Why?

5. Do I silently despise or dislike my significant other or spouse? How did it happen?

DEAD WEIGHT INTIMACY (DWI's)

There are some love affairs we need to drop. More specifically, we have relationships we need to end, stop, cancel, kill, and break away from. Loving them is draining us. Helping them is hurting us. We have done what we could. We have given what we had. We have cried till tears refuse to fall. We have bled till we're numb. There is no need for counseling because you would only be wasting the pastor's time. He's not going to change. She's not going to adjust. There is no reason to go to the altar and pray. The answer to your prayer is in your face everyday you deal with drama. The 2 of you don't match! Accept it! This man, this woman, this relationship is like a devil and it's time to exorcise our demons. Either they are leaving us or we are leaving them but make no mistake; one way or another, they are getting the HELL OUT OF OUR FACE!

This relationship is dead weight. You talk to your girlfriends about how unhappy you are. You drink with the guys after work because you as well as they know you don't want to go home. Your relationship is horrible. You know it. They know it and so does everyone else. So the million-dollar question everyone has on his or her mind is, "*If this crap is so bad, why in God's Green Earth are you still in it*". And while you give every reason in the book as to your rationale allow me to submit mine:

- The Sex Is Too Good

    Don't be surprised I said it because you know it's true. You are not happy with them. They embarrass you when you go out. They are inconsiderate to your feelings and your dreams. They don't care to hear your opinions but you love how they use what's between their legs. You love how you are sexed. This is not X-rated conversation. This is real talk. You know what it is. You fight with them. You argue with them. You cry. You get mad. Then you sex and all is well until the next event. You love the orgasms. You love the oral. How many times were you about to end the relationship and the sex changed your mind? How many times were you about to free yourself and the sex pulled you back in to the drama? My friend, you are enslaved to a passion and a fire incapable of sustaining you. The sex provided a temporary "honeymoon" period whereby we allowed ourselves to believe all is well when in actuality it was nothing more than a sexual band-aid for a core relational dysfunction. And many of us simply are not ready to leave the relationship because we don't want to forfeit the sex. Our intimacy with the person is dead. Our connection is severed but the sex is awesome. Hence, this is why we have some of the internal battles with ourselves as we do. Moreover, we are afraid the next man/woman we find will not be able to sexually satisfy us as the person we are with right now. We care about the person and though we know its over we use sex as a way to convince ourselves they still care about us. For some of us, it is precisely when we are having sex we feel empowered and in control. The sex is our throne.

And though we may feel powerless throughout the relationship, when we have sex we are powerful and a force to be reckoned with. And yet, there are others of us who use the good sex for another reason. The sex connects us to them and when we are denied sex, we feel abandoned, rejected, and alone. This feeling leads me to our next point.

- Fear Of Being Alone

Being alone is difficult for many people. As I stated before, all of us need to connect with people. When that connection isn't there, we quietly feel deprived of being human and we seek out ways to connect with something. The longer we're deprived, the stronger our need becomes. Soon we find ourselves in relationships taking us away from being ourselves and yet we can't understand why we can't break away from them. The truth is we are alone and we prefer to tolerate someone else's drama just so we won't have to continue being alone. Most of us are cringing while reading this line pertaining to our situation. We are masters at constructing our own context and rationale for justifying where our lives are but the rationale will not help us if we want to change. Our rationale merely serves as our excuse to do nothing and hope for something different. We are afraid of being alone. So we continue to remain involved in abusive relationships, our humanity continues to be reduced to that of being a sex object, and our lives remain meaningless and shallow.

- Hero Complex

The hero's complex is not considered in most circles as a psychological disorder as much as it is a person's overall disposition towards life. **It is the overwhelming compellingness to help other people even at the expense of one's own safety.** It usually develops as a response to something tragic or painful within someone's past. Consequently, the person feels compelled to never allow people to feel that kind of pain or experience that sort of tragedy believing his/her effort is the answer to those kinds of situations. Therefore, this is the difference between someone with a hero's complex and someone with a charitable heart for the one with charitable heart gives out of choice, not by mandate or obligation. The hero serves out of duty. The mandate of a hero is given to him/her by life, a deity, or assumes the responsibility for him/herself. The hero esteems the impact of his/her action beyond the scope of what it should be. Therefore, he/she is more prone to fall into self-delusionment, display extreme behaviors, and slide into such emotional lows like depression and anxiety. The hero complex walks hand-in-hand with having "control issues". Hence, it is difficult for the person with a hero's complex to accept the reality there are things we cannot control.

Where the hero complex affects our inability to walk away from unhealthy relationships is we believe we can save the person, even if it means destroying ourselves. We throw ourselves in harm's way believing that:

    a. We can handle whatever is coming our way.
    b. We can change the person.
    c. We can save our relationship.

While these intentions may be honorable, they

are not entirely our choice to make. First, we can only save our intimate relationships if both people involved give. The hero believes "*I can save this relationship by myself*". Simultaneously, the hero also believes if the relationship fails, it's his/her fault because he/she assumed a responsibility that was not his/her responsibility to assume alone. Consequently, the hero indirectly and subtlety excuses his/her partner of their responsibility in the relationship.

Moreover, both people must give 100% of what they have to the relationship and each other. The concept of **"*You give 50%, I give 50%*"** is a fallacy. It doesn't develop strong lasting relationships. It's a time waster. The 50/50 concept promotes the attitude "*you go first*". It waits on the other person to make a move and then the person waiting matches their effort. The 50/50 concept is nothing more than a useless game. It fosters distrust. It robs the couple of selfless initiative and it denies genuine intimacy. **Let's face it – relationships are risky business**. There are no guarantees. We don't know if the person we love today will change their mind tomorrow. We don't know if the same person we admire and respect today will be the same type of person next year. And we don't know if the person we married today will divorce us in 10 years. We don't get involved in intimate relationships to see what others can do for us. We give ourselves in relationships with the hope we will connect with someone who will give 100% of themselves to us as we give 100% of ourselves to them. With that said, the 50/50 concept does not work for us but against us and the hero complex does not help us but denies genuine partnerships which births the real intimacy we so desperately desire.

Secondly, heroes really believe they can change people. Yet reality is the responsibility of a person changing is left exclusively to the choice of the person in question. No one can change anyone else. We have a difficult time changing our own behavior so what makes the heroes believe they can change others? When people assume this kind of interpersonal relational posture, they have allowed themselves to slip into self-delusion. They give themselves more credit than they should. I cannot tell you how much I've seen my fellow Christians try to "save" others. Frequently, many believers confuse the "Christian Mandate" with the "Hero's Complex". The two are not the same. Jesus told his disciples,

> "*Go ye into all the world and preach the gospel to every creature. He that believeth and is baptized shall be saved: but he that believeth not shall be damned. And these signs shall follow them that believe; in my name shall they cast out devils, they shall speak with new tongues; They shall take up serpents; and if they drink any deadly thing, it shall not hurt them; they shall lay hands on the sick, and they shall recover*" (Mark 16; 15-18 KJV).

The attitude for the Christian is we are "vessels" for God used by God to execute God's will on earth as the Spirit of God enables us to do so. We do nothing on our own accord, except we willingly make a choice to allow ourselves to be available for God to use us. Outside of that choice, we can do nothing of positive impact in Jesus' name. Though we do feed the poor, help the helpless, clothe the naked and more; our attitude shapes the perception of our efforts as the "direct results" of God's Work. We see our work as the result of God's Hands. However, the hero's complex forces the heroes to believe the work of their hands is exclusively their work. We cannot allow ourselves to believe we have the power to change someone. We cannot. The more time we exert trying to champion someone else's change; we deny ourselves the maintenance we need in our own lives.

Finally, heroes believe they can handle more than they should. Many of us believe we are built to take a certain amount of pressure. While the notion is a true notion, most of us don't know where the line is drawn until we reach our limit. But for those of us who are heroes, we place ourselves in harm's way unnecessarily for the most admirable reasons. We are not invincible. We can be broken. We can be disappointed. We can get hurt and we can die. Some relationships we have carry a fatal element to them. Some have the ability to hurt us physically while others have the ability to kill our hopes, desires and dreams. Fatality is fatality. Whether emotional, mental, spiritual, social, sexual, or personal, the wrong type of relationship can severely wound if not kill one or more of those aspects of us.

STOP!

BREATHE DEEP! & CONSIDER!

1. Do I have a "Hero's Complex"? Why?

2. Why is it difficult for me to break away from relationships that hurt me?

3. What is it I really want when I have sex? Why?

4. What is it about being alone I'm truly fearful of? Why?

Moving beyond relationships to our dreams is a challenge. Whether they're quality relationships we need yet frustrating communicating the significance of our convictions or dead weight relationships draining life from us, we have to persevere through them to get to the prize – the tangible reality of our dreams. Like you, I even wrestle with it. As I write to you these very words, I wrestle with maneuvering through the intimacy issues, frustrating conversations, and coping with challenging relationships. There is no exact science to this. All of us are trying to figure out what works for us but the key to this life is to never stop trying. Because we have fallen seven times before does not guarantee the eighth time we try will result in the same way. Never allow what **_has_** happened to you dictate what **_can_** happen to you. What I can tell you my friend is this, "***When you feel the pressure of relationships trying to drain your focus and your excitement, let that very pressure serve as a reminder; the course you've charted to bring your dream to a tangible reality is the "right" course***". Yes my friend, pressure can serve as an indicator that you are traveling the right road. Be encouraged. You are closer to fulfilling what you set out to achieve.

Chapter 3
Personal Face Off

Take your time in answering these questions. It is difficult to come to grips with some of these answers and it will equally be difficult to discover the answers as well. Facing off with ourselves is not easy to do. Often times, we won't like what we see. People are always telling us who we are, what we do wrong, what we said wrong, how we hurt their feelings and more. And in some cases, their assessment about us is correct. Other times its wrong but it's up to us to discover for ourselves. Only when we truly know, can we truly change. If you are like me, it hurts you to know that you hurt your loved one. So let's look ourselves, question-by-question, let's record our answers and face off with ourselves to discover how to cope with frustrating conversations beginning with discovering who we are in relationships. Now my friend, let's write.

1. Have I asked people about who they truly are without asking myself was I ready to be responsible for what I heard?

2. What was my response?

3. What was their response?

4. Have many of my conflicts with others happened because of me misdiagnosing who I thought the person was compared to who they truly were?

5. Do I believe there is a value in discovering who people truly are? Why or why not?

6. Do I practice that conviction? How?

7. What are you "feeling" right now?

8. What are you thinking of right now?

9. What past or recent experiences make me crave being close to someone?

10. Do I spend more time fighting in my relationship than agreeing?

11. Which of the navigational concepts do I most relate to? Why?

12. Do I hold a quiet grudge against my significant other or spouse? What is it? Why?

13. Do I silently despise or dislike my significant other or spouse? How did it happen?

14. Do I have a "Hero's Complex"? Why?

15. Why is it difficult for me to break away from relationships that hurt me?

16. What is it I really want when I have sex? Why?

17. What is it about being alone I'm truly fearful of? Why?

CHAPTER 4

I Need More Than This (Church is NOT Enough)

*"A false balance is an abomination unto the Lord
but ajust weight is his delight"*
(Proverbs 11: 1 KJV)

In Yoga, "*balance*" and "*breath*" are captured into one word called "*Pranayama*". It is composed of two words "*prana*" meaning "*life-force*" and "*ayama*" meaning "*to lengthen or regulate*". Therefore, Pranayama means, "*to lengthen or regulate the life force*" or more literally translated "*breath control*". In Pranayama, 3 aspects are considered 1). Mechanics-the ability to move, 2). Metabolism-the ability to produce energy, and 3). Mentality-the ability to think & feel. The goal of Pranayama is to bring all of these facets into balance through breathing, meditation, and exercise. When balance is achieved, peace is achieved. When one of these areas are lacking, imbalance occurs manifesting internal or external conflict.

I must take time right now and applaud you for making it thus far. Chapter 3 was not easy. It was not easy for me to write and I'm sure it was not easy for you to read. Yet you did read it and you did engage yourself. You should give yourself a hug right now. Affirm yourself for a moment. If you don't learn to do it now, when will you take time to do it later? If you have a loved one near, spouse, child, or a relative, put this book down and give them a hug and a kiss. I have found some of the most meaningful moments of intimacy were random, spontaneous, unplanned moments that were simply seized to make a memory. I'M SERIOUS! PUT THE BOOK DOWN AND GO HUG AND KISS THEM!!!

Relationships are precious. They're frustrating too, but the good does out weigh the bad if we really take the time to count our blessings. So never forget to make some time to count them. Counting the blessings in our relationships truly does help keep a fresh perspective. It really does. This is another mile marker in your life's journey to Breathe Deep. As I'm sure you realize now, this is not a "how-to" book. This book walks with you as you live your life. It's here to make sense out of some of the most frustrating experiences and it coaches us along to remember what we have set out to achieve. This book reminds us of our perspectives and our commitment to respond to life differently than what we have done in times past.

Before I begin this chapter, I must explain why I wrote it. Vickie Winans did a remake of the gospel song *"Long as I got King Jesus"* and it caused me to really think. The words of the chorus are;

Long as I got King Jesus.
Long as I got King Jesus
Long, long, long as I got'em
I don't need nobody else

I began contemplating the notion I've heard countless times in sermons, songs and testimonies where the person would say, *"All I need is Jesus and I don't need no one else"*. It bothered me. I understand the general point of the statement but there was something more pressing on my mind and heart. I begin to fear that churches had slowly been advocating a gospel of closeness to God at the expense of minimizing the significance of healthy human relationships. I started observing wives jumping and shouting in church and inconsiderate of their husbands at home. I noticed husbands preaching in church all weekend but spending little to no time with their own children. Our ability to have healthy relationships with each other was quietly dissipating and no one seemed to know why. I constantly heard the devil blamed for the failure of marriages but he didn't stop us from being faithful to our vows – we did. The devil didn't stop us from playing with our children – we did. The devil did not decide for us the bad decision – we made those choices. We have neglected our relationships with others while we were claiming to have a relationship with God.

It was during this time of observation I read these words:

> "*And the LORD God said, It is not good that the man should be **alone**; I will make an help meet for him*" (Genesis 2; 18 King James Version).

Now I have mentioned this verse in a Chapter 1 regarding Eve and how she was the answer to Adam's insufficiency. But we must revisit this verse again for something more. I find it very interesting in the creation story God and Adam are together in perfection and God said Adam was still "alone". **If it is true when we sing songs like "*Long as I got King Jesus…I don't need nobody else*", why would God say that Adam was still alone when Adam was not alone, he had God?** It becomes apparent Adam needed more than just God. Adam didn't know he needed more because he believed he had all he needed, like we do in the songs we sing. Yet Adam did need more and God knew it. Adam needed God and he needed Eve. He needed his spiritual connection plus more. Most of us feel we need God but we feel we don't need each other. Thus our behavior has followed we have hurt ourselves by minimizing our opportunity to connect with others for better lives. Moreover, many of us have gone so far as to say we need church but we don't need anything else. For such reasons, many young men and women won't go to college because they are taught the classroom is against faith. Women are less empowered. Men are less informed. Opinion and interpretation are valued more than facts. People justify their behavior by claiming it's what God wants. If others don't behave as some of my fellow Christians believes, those people are attacked. This perspective is wrong. Church is good. It has its place and it's necessary but it is NOT ENOUGH! We truly need more than what church has to offer. And when we start living life beyond the walls of our churches, we will begin experiencing challenges like these…

OUTGROWING HOME

Church is a social institution that has been the bedrock of cultures for centuries. It has proven to have longevity through some of the most challenging and scrutinizing times. Specifically here in the States, many of us live, eat, and sleep church. It is part of are weekly activities. All of our families play a certain role in church. And if one thing is certain, you dare not miss a service, a Bible study, or Sunday school or you will be getting a phone call from somebody from somewhere soon. If your church were like mine (when I was kid), all the youth would sing in the choir, quote Easter speeches, participate in Easter egg hunts, do Christmas plays, attend vacation Bible school, and regularly attend Sunday school. And every now and again, one of us received the wonderful privilege of doing the Sunday morning youth sermon (usually that meant me and I was not enthused). Parents usually were equally involved wearing multiple hats. Some parents were the choir director and youth president while other parents were a musician and a trustee. Some were ministers while others were ushers. Church was always someplace where the entire family could come and really be a family.

Consequently, generations of family members continued to fellowship at the same church for years. You could sit on the same pew where your great grandmother or great-great grandfather sat. You could walk the hallways your mother walked when she was a little girl. You could sing in the choir stand where your aunts and cousins sang. And in some cases, you can even be where your mom and dad, grandmother and grandfather, aunt and uncle met, had their first kiss, said their first prayer together, and even got married. Church carries a wealth of heritage and history for us. While many of us can never find where our ancestry began, we at least have some ancestry to track in church.

Church was not only a place for family but also a safe haven to instill timeless values. We learned to wash our hands before eating. We learned to bow our heads and give thanks to God for food first.

We learned food was a blessing and people around the world were not as fortunate as we were. We learned the meaning of reverence. We were taught there are sacred things. They wouldn't allow us to run in the sanctuary. We were never allowed to play in the pulpit. We were taught God wants honesty. It was instilled in us to love each other (though some of us took it a little farther than I think our teachers intended). We were instructed to be obedient. These values are just a few that church served to impart into us.

 Our world-view was shaped in church. We were taught the Bible was the only book to contain the truth. We were educated Jesus walked on water, healed the sick, raised the dead and most importantly, he died for our sins and rose from the dead with all power in his hands. We were tested to know Jesus is God. We were told every other religion was a lie and Christians held the truth. If people did not confess Jesus, we were told they were going to Hell. Muslims were going to Hell. Jehovah's witnesses were going to Hell. A lot of people were going to Hell. Purgatory was a lie in Catholicism. Halloween was for the devil. We were told God's people were special and had special favor. Other people did not have God's Favor. We were taught if people didn't celebrate God like we did, sing like we did, dance like we did, then they really "didn't have it". We were taught women shouldn't wear pants in church and when they wore a dress coming above the knees that some shawl should cover their legs. These lessons shaped how we saw people growing up. Our conversations wrapped around these ideas. We adopted these notions to be accurate and unquestionable as children.

 And as it is in all things eventually - we grow up. We moved beyond what we were taught in order to discover the truth for ourselves. As kids, we adopted the values of our parents, teachers, and preachers as our own because that is what we knew and we had no other frame of reference to compare our lessons to. But as adults, we move to test and prove what we know to see if what we know is true and expedient. Usually around the time of graduation from high school our journey of self-discovery begins. Some of us chose the course of college and our faith came face-to-face with facts, philosophy, and research. Some of us enlisted in the military and we tested the values of our childhood against the politics of war. Some entered the job market where the demands of practical living clashed with the ideologies of what a relationship with God is supposed to be compared to what we were truly faced with. The bottom line for many of us became "*How do I reconcile the lessons and notions of my convictions with the difficult realities and facts of my experience*".

And for many of us, the question of connecting our convictions and values with our experience is precisely where we are in life right now. We are trying to figure out why the dots aren't adding up. We were taught they should connect but when we try the dots won't connect. We were taught prayer answers all things but there are plenty of questions we have no answers to. So we retreat back to the place where we were taught these ideas - church. And if you're like me, people in your church may have told you, "*God may not come when you want him, but he's always on time*" but our lights still got disconnected, the car still got repossessed, the marriage still ended in divorce, you still had the miscarriage, we still lost our jobs, and our hearts still became broken. So we question if the statement is true. We start questioning the validity of our brothers and sisters in the Lord. We wonder do these righteous, holy, upright, prayerful men and women of God really know what they are talking about because we have no answers and we tried it their way and we still have no answers. And while we have no answers we blame ourselves, we blame other people, and we blame God. And when we bring it to the clergy, ministers, preachers and teachers of our church, it becomes quite apparent, they don't really have answers either. Some tell us we're not praying hard enough. Some tell us we have to fast longer. Some tell us to meditate on a scripture. Others tell us to read more scriptures. Finally, once we jump through all of the religious calisthenics, we are left right back where we started. Only this time we are more frustrated, angrier, more confused, and feeling quite helpless. So when we return to them and give them the report, they hide behind the rebuttal "*Well, you know my brother and sister, the Lord works in mysterious ways*". And we are left standing in the midst of our life holding an empty bag with no answers as to why the bag we are holding is still empty.

And then something unexpectedly happens.

As we live our lives to do the best we can with the little we know, the little we know begins making sense to us and it starts working for us. We begin experiencing results. Not the way church people told us, but real results nonetheless. We start realizing our prayers are being answered. We start walking a walk that we weren't taught in Sunday school. We start experiencing blessings the preacher left out of his Sunday morning message. The Bible begins making sense as it pertains to our lives. We started reading for ourselves and started discovering truths contrary to the lessons we were taught. If you're like me, you may have heard some one tell you, "*Don't question God. Have faith and let God give you what God wants to give you. God is Sovereign. You're not. So don't question God*". However, when I started reading the scriptures for myself I discovered these words:

> "*Ask, and it shall be given you; seek, and ye shall find; knock, and it shall be opened unto you: For every one that asketh receiveth; and he that seeketh findeth; and to him that knocketh it shall be opened*" (Matthew 7; 6-7).

And here at this point, we begin to recognize something honest yet tragic. With all the history we may have at this church, our problem in relating to people may not be a matter of being a good Christian; it may merely be a matter of outgrowing home. And for some of us, that is precisely the case. WE HAVE OUTGROWN HOME.

So what are some of the indicators someone has outgrown their home church? Are there ways for me to discover if I am overstaying my welcome? Yes, there are some ways to tell if you have outgrown home though this is not an exact science. Let's explore 3 ways we can tell if we are outgrowing home.

1. Inactivity

We are bored! The preacher does not inspire us. The choir

sings us to sleep. We find ourselves gravitating towards the back and the aisle seats. This way when service is over we can exit quickly or if the service simply becomes unbearable we leave with little disruption. The message the preacher shares from the pulpit feels like a microwaveable meal 3 times heated over. It doesn't convict us. It doesn't challenge us. We don't want to get involved in church. And we find ourselves thinking about everything else but what we are there for. We present in body but absent in everything else. When the offering is taken, we are balancing our checkbooks. When the choir sings, we're thinking about the next episode of "Desperate Housewives". During the altar call prayer, we're trying desperately to not fall asleep. Some of us would go to sleep during that time but we're afraid of the embarrassment because we don't want anyone hearing us snoring when everyone says Amen. The bottom line for some of us is we have simply become bored with our church home. And that's because we've outgrown it.

2. Church-aholics

These types of people are equally on the same continuum with inactive people but just on the other side. We are just as bored as inactive people. The only difference between inactive people and us is where inactive people just sit; we throw ourselves into work – church work. We sing or direct the choir. We usher. We count the money. We play an instrument. We teach or preach. We could be the ones leading prayers and reading Scriptures. Whatever the case is, we have to be doing something in the church. Working in the church gives us identity. Working in church justifies our continued existence at the church because the truth is something we prefer not to deal with. For if we were to face the truth, the truth would be we are just as bored as inactive people AND WE FEEL GUILTY ABOUT IT!

We work in church out of our sense of Christian obligation. "God wills it; we work for the Lord" is many of our mentalities. We can't explain why we feel bored at church. And we are too afraid to tell anyone we are bored at church. So we seek to remedy the problem by becoming extremely engaged with church. Our rationale is to work out our boredom. For those of us who are stuck here, we believe if we can just work for the Lord, our boredom would leave. We say to ourselves what our grandmothers would say, "*an idle mind is the devil's workshop*". We convince ourselves that our own boredom is really the devil in disguise tricking us to forfeit our blessings. We never realize that our boredom is not the devil, but it is an indication we are not getting what we need to grow and be effective. We fight ourselves and the real devil is the guilt we have for feeling how we truly feel.

The devil of "guilt" will not empower us to face ourselves but causes us to work in places we truly don't believe in simply to save face. **Our guilt about our own feelings places a higher priority on satisfying other people's demands then facing our own fears**. People see our self-sacrificing actions esteeming us, as an example of what a true Christian man/woman should be while all the time we have the wrong motives. They can't see we are scared. They can't see we feel guilty about wanting to go to another church because we are not satisfied here. They can't see that inner conflict. And our guilt will not allow us to deal with our guilt. Our love for people isn't motivating our good works – guilt is! Hence, we live a LIE!!! Our lives become shallow. We have no substance. Actions are meaningless. We are nothing more than dead men and women walking,

> "Having a **form** of **godliness**, but denying the power thereof: from such turn away" (2 Timothy3; 5 King James Version).

Guilt is robbing us of our ability to be real and effective. Our ability to enjoy serving others is being stolen from us because of our inability to acknowledge our boredom and the causes therein. We will never find out why we are bored this way. We will never take action to overcome the boredom if we continue this route. We have outgrown our church home and we feel horrible about it. We feel we have betrayed our family. We feel we have betrayed our friends. We feel we have betrayed our loyalties, the place where our values were invested into us. We feel we are Judas. And in some cases, we feel like we, ourselves, are the devil for having such feelings. And if we don't face the reality that we have matured past where we are in our home church, we forever sentence ourselves to a life of pretense and lies because our guilt about our true feelings has incarcerated us. Break the chains of guilt! BE FREE! BE REAL! AND BE HONEST!

3. Trouble Maker

Those of us in this category can't seem to win for losing. We are seen as conflict starters, faithless, controlling, opinionated, jezebels and so forth and so on. People have pulled us off to the side to correct us, chastise us, advise us, and counsel us. We are seen as troublemakers. Most of us are completely clueless as to why we are seen in such a way. All we want is for people to advance in their faith and their lives. We see things that other people see and don't speak on or we see things other people really don't see. In both cases, when we speak up, it seems our insight is against what the church believes and one would think we just committed blasphemy or knowingly participated in some sacrilegious crime. Most of us don't know why this is happening to us but we do know that if something doesn't change either we will just shut up or we will leave.

The truth of the matter is we have outgrown home too. We are not in active. We are involved though some people would prefer us to go. We are not church-aholics. We do have a life outside of church. Yet the indication of our maturation is in the observations we make and the methodologies we take to achieve certain goals. We know women can wear pants and are in no danger of eternal damnation. We know women can preach. We see better ways of serving people but our ideas are in constant conflict with traditions and customs. We are constantly reminded, "that's not how it's done here. Your mama would be ashamed if she heard you say that. That's not how God wants it". It is not our goal to take over but to help. Nonetheless, we are called in for small prayer session with 2-4 people praying on us, as we are the topic of the prayer. They see us as the devil or an instrument of the devil. For many of us, we are tired of the "devil we bind you prayers" and the "God help them prayers". They pray on us as if we can't hear what they have to say. They don't see we are trying to help them not hurt them. And we are tired of being thrown to the wind for the sake of preserving the tradition as if their precious tradition was in jeopardy in the first place.

These kinds of experiences are indicators that we have outgrown home. We feel like we are traveling backwards every time we go to church, especially for women. In the professional world, women are managers, supervisors, CEOs, and executive directors and yet when you enter into the doors of the church, it feels like you leap backwards in time to a place where the highest status a woman could attain is motherhood. You feel stripped of your personhood and worth. You feel your contribution to humanity is minimized or ignored in church. You are a physician burdened daily with the difficult responsibility to inform families of the death of their loved ones and yet preachers and church folks tell you in church that you cannot preach the Word of Life. What madness is that? How can anyone rightfully justify such an opinion against such a practical reality? Will the same preacher not accept the announcement of his wife's demise from a female doctor? If so, we have the Word of God being used as a smoke screen to justify real male chauvinistic behaviors. Yet plenty of people do with no hesitation and no regard for anything else regardless of the case you or I make. These types of encounters, my friend, mean we have outgrown home.

STOP!

BREATHE DEEP! & CONSIDER!

1. Do you find yourself becoming bored or easily annoyed with your church? How can you tell?

2. Do you find yourself in conflicts or confrontations at church or about church often? What are your conflicts about?

3. Have you been the culprit attacking people because you are holding on to tradition rather than valuing them?

4. What are the issues that matter to you, which seemingly bother you greatly when in church? Why do those issues matter?

5. What are your values and what are the values of the church? Do they match?

6. Have your values or the church's values changed between the time you joined and now?

BIBLE SPITTERS

    This section is always an emotionally charged topic for me. It's been my experience some of the worst offenses I've ever experienced and seen were by people well versed in scriptures. They embarrassed me and humiliated others all in the name of declaring God's Word. I must say from the onset of this section, these types of people are DANGEROUS! They are dangerous because they mask their bitterness and jealousy behind the use of our source of greater influence and direction altogether. These people use Bible verses to justify spitting on your progress and minimizing your results. They are truly WOLVES IN SHEEPS CLOTHING!!!

There are many things I could say about "Bible Spitters" but it is necessary that we understand why these people are so dangerous. It is more than quoting the Bible to make us feel bad and justify their already wrong opinion. **The reason they are so dangerous to our ability to breathe deep in life is because we value the Bible as God's Word and they know that!** We don't see the Bible solely as a book. We don't value scriptures exclusively as a pericope of literature. We perceive the Bible as the written Words of God. We see those words as life, direction, consolation, and hope. When we feel alone, we read the Bible as a personal love letter from God assuring us God has not abandoned us. When we're broke, we read those words as God's promise to us that our lives will not remain as it currently is. The Bible is our direct link to God's Voice. When we read, we hear God. When we hear scriptures, we hear God personally addressing us. Therefore, the danger comes when "Bible Spitters" know how we value scriptures and use the Bible to incarcerate us. The secret is they are jealous of our success. They don't like how we our advancing. They don't understand how we can live the way we do while they are trapped in a state of stagnation. Consequently, they attack us like any other jealous, bitter, and vindictive person would. The only difference is they do it using scriptures. They believe God is speaking through them to correct us and ultimately stop us. They are convinced they hold the truth and we should listen. And if we are not careful, we will believe them because they are using the Bible (which is God's Voice to us) as their divinely authorized instrument to advocate their jealousy and displeasure of our progress and success in God's Name.

Our lives are too precious to be put on hold since someone is quietly bitter because we are doing what they wish they were doing. You cannot afford to forfeit your dreams because someone else won't put in the work like you've done to get what you have. So here are a couple of ways to identify and deal with "Bible spitters".

- **Avoid Them**

    Bible spitters are not interested in approaching a conversation with an open mind. Their minds are already made up. They know what they want to say. They know how they want to say it. They know why they want to say it. There is nothing new you can introduce them to because they're not open to anything new. Every answer you offer to a question they ask only draws more of your energy into a conversation designed to wear you down. So avoid them! When you see them, run. It does not mean you are afraid of them. It means you are aware of how they drain your energy and morale and you so choose to invest your effort in more profitable activity rather than entertaining their tiresome conversation.

- **Learn the Word**

    It is important that I define what I mean by the "Word". *The Word is the spirit of inspiration behind the written words in the Bible.* Quite often, we use the terms "Word of God" and "Bible" interchangeably. However, God did not come down and write the Bible, humanity did. Men wrote the Bible by inspiration. So when we read scriptures looking for God's Voice and direction, we read the written words while anticipating the spirit of inspiration to speak to us equally. When we say the Bible is alive, what we really are referring to is the inspirational spirit BEHIND the words has ministered to our hearts in real time. Though the written words were penned hundreds of years ago, the inspirational spirit of why the words were written in the first place keeps them alive. *When we connect with the spirit of the words in the Bible, we also connect to the same inspiration motivating the writers of yesteryear to write.* It is by this connection we call the Bible "The Word of God" because we are reading age-old words simultaneously experiencing real time meanings, current significance and personal impact application. It is for these reasons we value scriptures so preciously.

So the reason why we must learn the "Word" is because Bible spitters know the Bible. They know what the written words say, hence, why they quote book, chapter and verse. Bible spitters don't understand the spirit of inspiration behind the written words. And they don't care to know either. Consequently, while the general intent of utilizing Scriptures is to inspire, motivate, lead, direct, inform, enlighten, reprove, confirm and even discipline; Bible spitters use the Bible to accomplish the end of wounding, offending, hurting, harming, destroying, and minimizing. They are destructive in their use of the Bible. Therefore, we must be read the Bible looking to hear "the Words of God" for our lives. **When we know what the spirit of inspiration is in the words, Bible spitters can't insult our progress because we have learned the secret to the Bible, which is, reading the written words and hearing the inspirational spirit.**

It is imperative we learn how to identify Bible spitters. There are some common traits among these types of dream destroyers. Let's expose some character identifiers.

- **They are REALLY, Really, really - RELIGIOUS.**

    Bible Spitters are the most religious people we will ever meet. They have a Bible verse for everything. If the car doesn't start – quote a Bible verse. If the baby is crying – quote a Bible verse. If the food is burnt – quote a Bible verse. Everything that happens, they have a Bible verse for. They are in church often. They know all the gospel songs. They know all the popular preachers. They're in all the prayer meetings. And they know all the gossip (but we won't go there). However, the twist behind the super-religious person is he/she knows the information but falls short in continual practice. They preach good words but practice little of their own words (if at all). They spend an overwhelming amount of energy pointing out the flaws in others by way of Bible verses but refuse to use one-quarter of the same energy to see themselves. They portray such a close relationship with God but have a horrible relationship with people.

- **They are REALLY, Really, really SELF-IMPOSING.**

    Bible Spitters never mind their own business. Any opportunity they have to approach you in order to "help" you, they will. It doesn't matter the source of information or the credibility of what they hear. Whether the information came by way of gossip, hearsay, or eavesdropping - all they want is **opportunity** to invite themselves into your business and your life. Do not be afraid to stand up for yourself. Your life is your life. You are responsible for it. It's your business – not theirs. **So as they seek to offer unwelcomed advice on your life via Bible scriptures and church talk, politely yet firmly inform them when their services are needed – you'll ask for it.**

- **They are REALLY, Really, really INCONSIDERATE.**

    Bible spitters are like bullies. They will pick with you on the basis that you are a "**babe in Christ**". Translation: "*You don't know what God has for your life but I do*" or "*you're too immature for the things of God but I'm* *not*". They are self exalting at our expense. They feel justified in minimizing our experiences and they use their experiences as lessons to teach us as if 1). We need them to actually teach us and 2). As if we can't learn from our own experiences. Bible spitters talk to us as if we're stupid. And though many of us may not have been in church as long as they have or know as many Bible verses as they know, we must remember we have just as much to contribute as they do. We must remember church is not the place for competition but collaboration. We cannot allow Bible spitters to egg us into a competitive attitude justifying, validating, and vindicating experiences that need not be justified, validated or vindicated. All of us have experiences and some of those experiences will differ while others are similar but ALL OF OUR EXPERIENCES ARE IMPORTANT!

- **They are REALLY, Really, really SELF DECEIVED.**

Bible spitters believe they are God's Spokesmen/women for humanity. The basis of their conviction is they know the Bible. They feel authorized in telling us about our lives. You may have heard a Bible spitter start a conversation like this, "*God said…*" or "*The Bible says…*" or my personal favorite, "*The Lord told me to tell you*". They don't think they can be wrong because they have convinced themselves God is speaking through them and it is impossible for God to be wrong. They claim the "Spirit of God" is using them and they are so powerless to what they say. IT'S A LIE. They are not puppets on God's string. They are human beings who make choices like the rest of us. There is no "hocus pocus" here though there are some Bible Spitters who will go so far as to put on a show for us. They put on a show to make us believe they're actually experiencing a supernatural encounter before/after their divine message is delivered. Some pretend to fall into a trance. Others choose to act mystical and speak as an Oracle of God, yet when you ask them, they pretend like they can't remember what happened. The truth is they have deceived themselves and if we are not careful, they will deceive us too.

We cannot entertain conversations with self-deceived individuals. It's a futile effort. The commonality between the 2 people in the conversation is non-existent. They feel their words are God's words. There is no debate in the matter for them. So the only possible result in continued interaction with Bible spitters is we'll become stagnant in the pursuit of our dreams and ultimately stop altogether. Then we'll become bitter and deceive ourselves too and then we'll attack others as were once attacked. Therefore, we must be cautious in who we entertain conversation with. The right kinds of conversation will enhance, but conversations with Bible Spitters will drain us.

STOP!

BREATHE DEEP! & CONSIDER!

1. Have your conversations been draining recently? Why do you think this is the case?

2. Have you been quietly frustrated by conversations with people you thought were close to God? Why?

3. Do you know any "Bible Spitters"? What are their names?

4. Are you a Bible spitter? How did you become this way?

I Need More Than This

Do you want to change?

5. How do you feel when someone quotes & relates Bible verses to your personal situation?

6. What are you thinking when someone tells you that you are wrong and uses Bible scriptures to prove their point? Why?

___

Now it is important I share this with you here. I firmly believe people can speak to us by inspiration and their words directly impact our current situation. We need those types of people. They up lift us and cause us to believe we can achieve and be successful. These people empower us to breathe deep when we feel we're drowning in shallow meaningless situations. However, I will not excuse people who use the Bible for promoting their personal agendas and hidden motives selling the pitch as if it's a "Word from God". These people kill our hopes, annihilate our dreams, and violate our convictions and they use our precious convictions as the means to do so. We must not let ourselves be dooped by the cunningness of Bible spitters. Avoid them. Stay true to our perspectives and committed to our dreams. This life is your life. <u>YOU CONTROL IT! THAT POWER IS YOURS.</u>

<u>DAMNED TO HELL</u>

I cannot tell you how many times people have sent me to hell. Bible spitters have minimized my own Christian experiences because I was not a Christian according to their understanding of what a Christian should be. If my conversation or actions didn't mirror what churches had continually set as the general attitude for life, I was considered a hypocrite, a pretender, and a reprobate. I have attended other churches where the same conversation and lifestyle empowered Christians to be themselves and love God freely. Those people serve others out of compassion and love God out of heartfelt conviction rather than fear and anxiety. Therefore, I came to quickly discover people are different wherever I go and churches are no different. I discovered while people change from place to place I must be consistent in my convictions, perspectives and be true to who I am. I learned to BREATHE DEEP only when I habitually practiced those discoveries, regardless of where I found myself physically.

The word "hell" is mentioned 52 times in the King James Version of the Bible. Therefore, it's a good idea I give just a little attention to this word. Plenty of people readily reference this word and have no clue as to what it means. Some have even raised the question, "*What is hell*". While some theologians argue it to be a literal place and others a metaphorical place, they all agree hell is a place of torment. In hell, there is pain, abandonment, and it is a low place. Nothing good resides there and escape from hell only comes about by someone else's help, particularly God's help. Therefore, when people condemn us to hell what it means is people want us tormented, abandoned, hurting, consumed by sadness, depressed, with no escape except from God. They want us punished. They want us judged and in sending us to hell, they presume upon themselves the authority to judge us, sentence us, and condemn us. Yet, there is only one who commands the authority to send us to hell.

> "*I am he that liveth, and was dead; and, behold, I am alive for evermore, Amen; and have the keys of **hell** and of death*" (Revelation 1: 18 KJV).

So while it is now clear what hell is, we must discuss why so many churches choose to condemn us there. Unfortunately, the answer is simple. **Our lives are rebelling against church people's perspective of life.** We are doing more than what traditions empowered us to do. Women are accomplishing more in society. Our success is crossing religious lines impacting other areas of life, which are considered taboo by church folks. They condemn us to hell because they feel our lives are against what God wants. Our lives are labeled rebellious against God. They believe their opinion is God's final answer. But on the contrary, we are not rebellious against God. **We have decided to make our life count in every area and we offer no apologies for our success**! God is not displeased with us, church folks are. We are doing what they preach about. We are living what they sing about. We are eating the blessings they read about. They are damning us to hell but we are blessed with heaven's kiss.

Many churches, pastors, and congregations are simply "behind the time". It is not that they are ignorant to the changes of society. It is not that they are unaware of the times. They simply refuse to change. It is easier for the world to be wrong and they are right. It is easier to call everything they don't do sin than to reconcile the difficulty of truly living. Consequently, so many churches preach against people whose lives don't fall into the prescribed way of living as spelled out by their interpretation of the Bible and their established traditions. This course of action indirectly (and very directly at times) damns us to hell according to their perspective. They waste no time expressing such a notion. They say to us that a Christian shouldn't be involved in a fraternity or sorority. They preach against R & B artists who give God thanks for success in their careers. They make the argument R & B artists should give their gift to God assuming Gospel music isn't just as conniving and deceitful (if not more). They are misled and misinformed. Now I must be clear on this matter. I am not condemning churches who hold fast to their traditions. There is nothing wrong with being faithful to what you know. However, when churches attack individuals because their advancements supersede traditional expectation, that church is wrong. There is no excuse for ministries being fanatical in their condemnation of others merely because they have succeeded beyond traditional attitudes. We will not accept churches condemnation of our success. We will not allow them to damn us into torment, abandonment, and pain. We have come through too much in our lives to allow non-invested, mentally limiting, religious folks steal our fire. Don't forfeit your dreams. Keep them alive. WE MAY BE DAMNED TO HELL IN THEIR EYES BUT WE ARE BLESSED IN GOD'S!

STOP!

BREATHE DEEP! & *CONSIDER!*

1. Can you recall a time you felt attacked in church because of your views or convictions? What happened?

2. What are 2 ways you wanted to respond? Be Honest.

3. Have you damned anyone to hell? Why?

MAINTAINING A FRESH PERSPECTIVE

It is here in our conversation we must revisit what we discussed in Chapter 1. We must remember the difference between **context** (what happens to us) and our **perspectives** (our responses to what happens to us). Life happens. We can't change the events of our lives once they happen. We must remember to accept the fact that they happened and move on. We must keep in mind while we cannot control the past we can control our response to it. It is our individual responses to each event that inevitably culminate into our perspective. Therefore, we must control how we respond. If we are not careful, we can easily slip back into the shallow lifestyles and engage once again into the meaningless routines prior to picking up this book. Dealing with religious folks can be draining in ways beyond expression. So we must maintain a fresh perspective.

Church is a special topic for us. It's special because we value church in so many ways. Some of us see it as our service to God. Others see it as the place we hear from God. Yet there are others who attend out of habit and tradition. Regardless of why many of us attend church, it is vital we remember why church exists. I do not presume to have the ultimate definition for why church exists. However, I have defined it in my life and that definition has helped me keep my perspective fresh when dealing with Bible Spitters, being damned to hell, and outgrowing home. **"The Church" is the moral consciousness of the community.** If injustice is roaming free, the church should call for justice. If hatred roars its voice like a lion, the church should whisper the soft words of compassion. Against a world of liars and deceivers, the church is a place of integrity. Against pain and oppression, the church is a safe haven. We expect to be inspired, compelled, and directed in church. Our spirits anticipate encouragement when we come to church. And when we do wrong, there should be a presence within the church convicting us of our actions and attitudes, even when no one knows our secret crimes and hidden violations. The Church is the voice of reason, the champion of justice, and the advocate of rightness. This is what church is for (as I have defined it for myself).

With this perspective, we understand our spiritual development will happen in church and yet there is so much more we need than just church. We do not simply have spiritual needs only but we have emotional, intellectual, social, physical, environmental, and even sexual needs as well. This is the single point of this chapter. **We need more than church in order to "breathe deep"**. If we limit our development to church, then we'll have missed our opportunity to live an optimal life. Everything we need to achieve cannot be done in church. Everything we need to be developed cannot be cultivated in church. And everything we want cannot be found in church. We need church. And we need more than church too.

Now I applaud those people who have stepped up the service of their ministries beyond the traditional role. Some churches have day cares, elementary schools, recreation centers, skating rinks, and even colleges. I know churches that have apartment complexes and workout facilities. And while all of these extensions of service help impact more people, churches and the people thereof still have the mandate to be the **consciousness of the community**. Doing all of these other things only create wider ranges of opportunity to achieve that purpose (as I have defined it). Churches are not vacuums but outreach centers. We reach out to individuals, families, communities, and even cities sharing a message of hope, good news, and direction for the purpose of inspiring people to live better. The idea of church does not have to be seen as a competitor with other entities in the community. Collaboration is pivotal to success. As long as we (meaning churches) continue to attack potential partners, we'll continually isolate and reduce our chances to have significant impact in the areas we can't reach. Here's the bottom line: CHURCHES CANNOT DO EVERYTHING! We cannot employ every person. We cannot educate every child. We cannot do everything. There is much we can do and that which we can do, we should do. However, there is equally much we CANNOT do. And with that which we cannot do, we can collaborate. And while I hear many of my brothers and sisters say," God can do all things", the truth is WE ARE NOT GOD! Let's let God do what God needs to do and we do what we need to do. Let us build relationships and stop the fanatical attacks of the past. Let us accept the fact people will believe differently as we believe. Let us keep a fresh perspective when we outgrow home, encounter Bible Spitters, and damned to hell. Let us expand our lives past the walls of tradition and religion. Let us together BREATHE DEEP OR DIE SHALLOW alone!

YOU MAY NOW TURN THIS PAGE…

AND LET'S ACHIEVE REAL BALANCE!!!

Chapter 4
Achieving Balance

I started this chapter off quoting a Bible verse discussing true balances versus false balances. I shared with you Yoga information regarding when balance is achieved, peace is achieved and when balance is not achieved, conflict occurs. Looking throughout church history, conflict has been apparent. From Christian crusades to tele-evangelical financial scams, we have seen the results of conflict from being without balance. Yet there are also countless other examples where we see peace achieved when churches achieved balance. They invested in life around them rather than operating as a vacuum. Our perspective will determine our action. If we aim to value church for its contribution without minimizing the contributions of others around us, we can achieve balance and peace individually and collectively. But if we continue to believe *"all we need is Jesus and we don't need nobody else"*, then we are sentencing not only ourselves, but also generations to follow a life of conflict and pain with the hope they find their own way without our help. Therefore, take this time to write the answers to the questions we posed before. Take your time and let's achieve balance together. Now STOP, BREATHE DEEP, and WRITE.

1. Do you find yourself becoming bored or easily annoyed with your church? How can you tell?

2. Do you find yourself in conflicts or confrontations at church or about church often? What are your conflicts about?

3. Have you been the culprit attacking people because you are holding on to tradition rather than valuing them?

4. What are the issues that matter to you, which seemingly bother you greatly when in church? Why do those issues

matter?

5. What are your values and what are the values of the church? Do they match?

6. Have your values or the church's values changed between the time you joined and now?

7. Have your conversation been draining recently? Why do you think this is the case?

8. Have you been quietly frustrated by conversations with people you thought were close to God? Why?

9. Do you know any "Bible Spitters"? What are their names?

10. Are you a Bible spitter? How did you become this way? Do you want to change?

11. How do you feel when someone quotes & relates Bible verses to your personal situation?

12. What are you thinking when someone tells you that you are wrong and uses Bible scriptures to prove their point? Why?

13. Can you recall a time you felt attacked in church because of your views or convictions? What happened?

14. What are 2 ways you wanted to respond? Be Honest.

15. Have you damned anyone to hell? Why?

CHAPTER 5

YES!!! FINALLY!!! (Tasting Small Success)

*"For I know the **thoughts** that I think toward you, saith the LORD, **thoughts** of peace, and not of evil, to give you an expected end"* (Jeremiah 29: 11 King James Version).

It can be difficult to breathe in a room of smokers when you're a non-smoker. We know we need to breathe, but breathing is difficult and unpleasant. The more smoke that's in the air, the more difficult it is to breathe. We try to find pockets of clean air, but those pockets are only there for a brief moment, only to quickly collapse with smoke. We struggle and struggle to find clean air until we can't take the environment anymore and we need a change. We focus our minds on one place – the door. We know on the other side of the door what we need is there – fresh, clean air. So we make moves. We move around people. We limit our conversations. People call us but we keep moving. We focus on breathing. We breathe intentionally. We don't lose sight of the door. We press and press. It becomes more difficult the closer we get to the door because as we aim to go out, so many more people are coming in. We step on people's feet by accident. We bump people's shoulders unintentionally. Some people see us as rude but we don't have time to be preoccupied by their opinion, we need to breathe. And once we break <u>through the door to the other side – WE CAN BREATHE DEEP!!!</u>

This chapter is precisely what it feels like to get to the other side of the door. This is the chapter where fresh, clean air is. We fought through the smoke of chapters 1-4. We offended some people, ignored some people, and limited our contact with some people. We sat down and thought about what we really wanted. We moved quickly to get it. We focused our efforts, energies and attentions to achieve those goals. We took direct action. We got tired. We became rejuvenated. We received help. It got harder the closer we came. We never quit. And now we can honestly say to ourselves – SUCCESS!!!

There is nothing sweeter than tasting our hard-earned success. It doesn't matter how people measure our success. To us, our success is HUGE! Those who choose to measure our success don't know the prices we had to pay, the relationships we walked away from, or the sacrifices we made to get this far. AND TO US, IT DOESN'T MATTER! We know about the nights of frustration, the days of scrambling, and the heated meetings. We are familiar with the critics and the skeptics. We've heard everyone's opinion and how right everyone else is. But this success right here – IS OURS AND NO ONE CAN STEAL THIS FROM US. THIS PLACE IS A GOOD PLACE!!!!

THROW A PARTY

There is no question about it. This is celebration time. You have solidified your effort and energy and it has paid off. This is the time when you call your friends, call your loved ones, and call those who have helped you, even call those who sat on the sidelines and – THROW A PARTY!!! My friend, this is not a suggestion. Throwing a party is a MUST! You must celebrate this accomplishment because it shows that your life is really changing. It shows that all the stuff in your head was more than just a good idea. Throwing a party proves that your conversation was really a declaration of things to come. It shows others and confirms with yourself that you really were making moves. Throwing a party really does display you weren't talking off the cuff about big ideas and grand dreams that would amount to nothing. YOU'VE DONE WHAT YOU SAID YOU WOULD DO AND NOW YOU'RE THROWING A PARTY TO PROVE IT!!!

Throwing a party has such significance for everyone involved. First, it has special significance to you. Let's face it; this journey was no cakewalk. To work through the issues, the fights, the disappointments, and the broken promises and to arrive at the place where you desired to be nonetheless is simply AWESOME! Throwing a party is where you kiss yourself and say, "*I knew you could do it*". This is where you embrace yourself and say, "*Thank you, for not giving up on me*". Celebrating us is something we hope others would do but the truth is we need to do it for ourselves. It doesn't mean we are beyond others celebrating us because that would be a lie. But it does mean we have to value ourselves first. Look at this way, who knows about your sacrifices better than you? Who knows about the secret internal conflicts you had with yourself better than you? Who knows when you wanted to quit better than you? I think you get my point. Who can better celebrate you better than you? Quite often, we want people to know about the stuff they can never humanly know about. And then we get mad with them when they don't appreciate us the way we feel they should. They can't. Their ability to appreciate us is premised off of what they really know. And let's be honest, as close as some people are to us, they can never truly know how we feel about something no matter how many times we discuss it. They weren't the direct recipients of the impact – we were. So it's foolish to expect people to celebrate us like we would celebrate ourselves. They didn't make our investment - we did. For this reason alone, we must celebrate ourselves.

Secondly, throwing a party is one of our ways to say thank you to the people who invested in us. We weren't successful by ourselves. We had help. Adam got help from Eve. Jesus had help carrying his cross from Simon. And we had help from a number of people. Just like we desire to be celebrated they need to be celebrated too. "Thank you" goes a long way. Sometimes the difference between people doing the same thing over and over again and taking it to the next level could simply be in someone appreciating them for what they've done. As a district executive with the Boy Scouts of America in Cleveland, OH, I learned the power of "Thank You". The 1st year of my fundraising campaigns, I had no clue what I was doing. I had very little help, but we superseded our goal by nearly 120%. I threw a party to say thank you to all the people that helped me. The following campaign season all of those people returned and most of them raised twice the dollar amount in less than half the time. Saying, "thank you" works.

Parties are great ways to reconnect with your friends and allies.

You can get their feedback easily. You can talk to them and discover what were their struggles as they invested in you. **Remember, your success is also the success of others who helped you.** Just as you were going through challenges and addressing issues, so were they. It's easy to be consumed in our own problems and forget that the others helping us have problems too. Throwing a party provides us the opportunity to talk to them and discover what they went through. It's so important that we hear their story as it pertains to them helping us. It's an atmosphere where they can candidly talk about the struggles without feeling saddened because the party itself is proof their investment was worth it. Yet, your interest in them will create a greater sense of loyalty because you aren't concerned about the benefits they offer toward your goal; you're concerned about building a stronger relationship.

Thirdly, throwing a party is our opportunity to further build our team. **Let's be honest; everyone wants to be on a winning a team.** People want to be connected with other successful people. I discovered one of the main reasons I had a hard time securing help doing things was because it was my first time doing it. People had no track record to go by, except my word. And while I would like to think I'm a man of my word, strangers don't know me or the value of my word. However, once success is attained and they know about it, it's easier to recruit people to on the next go round. This is our opportunity to bring in fresh blood. People stand on the sidelines for many reasons, but one of those reasons is fear. They are afraid of disappointment. Most of us have been disappointed in some way. We remember how disappointment feels. They don't want to experience that again, either. So they stand on the sidelines until the 1st game is won. Suddenly, they're inspired and they want to play. Throwing a party is key to reconnecting with the potentials on the sideline.

Throwing a party is a win-win for everyone. We can celebrate ourselves, rejuvenate our friends, and recruit new allies. Everyone feels they have won and rightfully so. There is no such thing as isolated success. All of our success was connected to someone else. We must never lose sight of that. The more we keep our relationships healthy, the greater our successes will be in the future. Congratulations on achieving your goal. Now put this book down and go THROW A PARTY!

STOP!

BREATHE DEEP! &   CONSIDER!

1. Pick a date far enough out in advance where the likelihood of someone not coming to the party is minimized.

2. Invite everyone who has invested in you like friends, allies, and people who have heard and not heard about what you've achieved.

3. Allot time to recognize those who directly contributed to your success. People love public kudos.

4. Be Mobile. Let someone else structure the party so you can move around and talk to people. People want to see you. Let someone else have the responsibility of the party. Remember, this is YOUR NIGHT!

THE JUDGING EYE

Let's face it; there are people who don't want to see us happy. They don't care about our success. They don't care about the party. They want us miserable and we know who those people are. Some people say they're like that because they're jealous of our progress. Some say they're mad because they're not "doing" what we are. Others say they're just having a bad day. And yet others say they are merely just that way. Whatever the reasoning for their psychological disposition towards us, one thing is certain – THEIR ISSUES ARE NOT OUR PROBLEMS. So don't adopt them. Don't waste your time trying to figure out why they don't like you or why they have something negative to say. It's their problem, not yours. Don't make it your problem.

Successful times can be just as dangerous (if not more dangerous) as being in the process. They're deadly because when we are successful, all eyes are on us compared to when we were in the process, some people didn't even know we existed. Success attracts all kinds of attention. It attracts believers who want to know the secrets of your success. They will incorporate our advice into their plans. Success attracts disbelievers because it gives them something new to say something negative about. Disbelievers will attack success when they know nothing about it and here's a reality check – THEY DON'T NEED TO KNOW ANYTHING ABOUT IT! Their ignorance is their weapon. Their ignorance is the fuel that drives their gossip and their negativity. They will attack us. They will minimize our success with their words. And I say, LET THEM!

My friend, you are successful now. You don't have to defend your work. Let your work defend itself. Now that all eyes are on you, your behavior is under scrutiny. To defend your work (in some but not all cases) will be perceived as if your success was established without integrity. Remember, the attacks you're experiencing are the results of your accomplishments, not toward you personally. So when you are attacked, point them back to the accomplishments and DON'T TAKE IT PERSONAL! Did you hear me? DON'T TAKE IT PERSONAL! They don't know you personally. So there's no need to get offended. Now this is easier to say than do for one reason. You invested your soul into your success. So while I say we must not take the attacks personally we equally understand that our success does have personal significance to us. We must not confuse the two. Maintain your personal satisfaction, but don't take what they have to say personally.

There is another secret we must know about the judging eye. Their attacks will ignite responses from our allies, particularly those who have invested in our success like us. This is where we must manage our team. We must remind our team that the attacks are really against our success and not against us. Therefore we must remain disconnected though our success has personal significance. We have recruited our teams. They know us. They trust us. They believe in us. They love us. And they look to us for leadership, so we must lead. And here's the catch, our team will become even more upset with the attacks because they know the caliber of men and women we are. This is why it will be so important we lead with **humility** and **sobriety** because our team will be ready to pounce on anyone who says something negative about us, if we let them. Moreover, the sideline people are watching too. They are wondering how will we deal with the drama. Our actions will determine their level of confidence in us. So we must be mindful of ourselves, our team, and those who stand by watching. Our future success depends on what we do here.

STOP!

BREATHE DEEP! & CONSIDER!

1. What are some attacks you've responded positively to? Why?

2. What are some attacks you've responded negatively to? Why?

3. How have these attacks affected your team?

4. How did you manage your team?

KEEP IT MOVING

Achieving success is great. It's a wonderful feeling to set goals and accomplish them. Success is intoxicating. Cranberry and Grey Goose, Cognac, White Russian, or an Amaretto Sour on the rocks has nothing on the taste of success. Yet, the danger of being intoxicated with success is that we stop making progress. We are caught up in the hype of the moment and never move past it to the next goal. Intoxication with success causes us to lose touch with reality. It leads us to believe we have arrived, when in the scope of our ultimate goals, we are only few mile markers closer. Therefore, it behooves us to keep our progress moving forward.

Many of us get caught up in throwing the party and never get back to work. We want to celebrate our beginning and talk about what we'll do next. The only problem is we never get back to doing what we did to become successful in the first place. We must let go of our success and focus our eyes to the next goal in mind. There is a Bible verse that says:

> "*No, dear brothers and sisters, I have not achieved it, but I focus on this one thing: Forgetting the past and looking forward to what lies ahead*" (Philippians 3:13 New International Version).

While this verse is speaking about attaining a perfect relationship with Christ, there is a principle all can benefit from here. The principle is **"Forget the past – Focus on the future"**. I don't mean forget the past as if it is insignificant. I do mean accept whatever happened in the past and move on. Quite often, we only want to forget the negative experiences of our history and dwell on the positive. That way of thinking is still paralyzing because while we are dwelling on the positive, we are steadily missing present opportunities to make new memories. We'll continue that course of action until we find ourselves wishing for the "good old days". The same good old days we intentionally deleted out the bad days from. Consequently, we find ourselves romanticizing a period in time that in reality never was like the way we tell it. For this reason, we must let go of both, our failures and our successes, in order to effectively move to the next goal.

We must also keep it moving so we don't develop self-destructive behaviors. For the sake of this conversation, I'll simply define **self-destructive behaviors** as "*the conscious or subconscious habits developed by which impairing one's ability to effectively advance*". In other words, we stop our own progress. We can stop our own progress intentionally by just believing we have arrived when we haven't. We can stall our progress unintentionally with habits we have developed that we didn't realize were habits. We have addressed the intentional stuff but we need to take a closer look at the unintentional self-destructive habits.

Dr. Michaele Dunlap, clinical psychologist, keys into something quite significant concerning self-destructive behaviors. She says,

> "*As women we are especially vulnerable to self destructive behavior which has its roots in the sense of shame. Because we are sometimes ashamed of the simple fact of being women*" (http://www.oregoncounseling.org/ArticlesPapers/Documents/SelfDestructBehavMD.htm).

The power of shame is an overwhelming reality. Though Dr. Dunlap was speaking of shame as it directly affects women, there is a definite connection between the feeling of shame and guilt and self-destructive behaviors. This is where some of our unchallenged behaviors throughout chapters 1-4 begin surfacing themselves now. Our success is now public. People see what we have achieved. And some would like to make us feel guilty for it. They would like to transition our success from being good to being wrong. That is the danger of the judging eye. They will aim to make us see what they want us to feel. They want our success to be translated into our shame because they have not done what we have. If we don't struggle with the problem of "**people pleasing**", then we're fine. But for those of us who do, we are at risk. We are at risk because our habits constantly have us gauging the satisfaction of people versus our own satisfaction. If people are satisfied, we move forward. If people are not, we feel ashamed and stop. Consequently, we give the power of living our own lives into others' hands. This is a self-destructive habit in itself. Control of our lives and the value of our own opinion is what we must reclaim. In order to BREATHE DEEP, we must divorce ourselves from the control of public opinion and empower our own voice! Value yourself, my friend. Esteem yourself worthy for your next level of success greatly depends on you being able to do this.

STOP!

BREATHE DEEP! & CONSIDER!

1. Have you felt guilty about your accomplishments lately? Why?

2. Is it easy for you to become intoxicated with your success? Why do you think that is?

3. Do you think some of your habits impair your progress? What are some of those habits?

4. Are you a people pleaser? Why do you think that is? Do you think you can change?

Chapter 5
Staying Focused

Success is good. We need to celebrate when we achieve but it's not the end. There is always the next goal to accomplish. Therefore, we must remain focused. Let's continue to self-authorize ourselves by writing answers to these questions and taking heed to some of these recommendations. We are BREATHING DEEP now but we must continue to breathe deep **consistently with intent** so these moments can become healthy habits. So stop reading, take a deep breath, and write.

1. When was the last time you threw a party?

2. Pick a date far enough out in advance where the likelihood

of someone not coming to the party is minimized.

3. Invite everyone who has invested in you like friends, allies, and people who have heard and not heard about what you've achieved.

4. Allot time to recognize those who directly contributed to your success. People love public kudos.

5. Be Mobile. Let someone else structure the party so you can move around and talk to people. People want to see you. Let someone else have the responsibility of the party. Remember, this is YOUR NIGHT!

6. What are some attacks you've responded positively to? Why?

7. What are some attacks you've responded negatively to? Why?

8. How has these attacks affected your team?

9. How did you manage your team?

10. Have you felt guilty about your accomplishments lately? Why?

11. Is it easy for you to become intoxicated with your success? Why do you think that is?

12. Do you think some of your habits impair your progress? What are some of those habits?

13. Are you a people pleaser? Why do you think that is? Do you think you can change?

CHAPTER 6

NO!!! THIS CAN'T BE HAPPENING! (Setbacks)

"Although the fig tree shall not blossom, neither shall fruit be in the vines; the labour of the olive shall fail, and the fields shall yield no meat; the flock shall be cut off from the fold, and there shall be no herd in the stalls: Yet I will rejoice in the LORD, I will joy in the God of my salvation" (Habakkuk 3: 17-18 King James Version).

[1]Hyperventilation is abnormally fast and deep breathing resulting in the loss of carbon dioxide from the blood, thereby causing a decrease in blood pressure[1]. Typically it's caused by anxiety. Tingling sensations in the toes and fingers, dizziness, and loss of consciousness are just a few of the results of hyperventilating. When people experience such a breathing disorder, they usually feel out of control and helpless. They breathe so fast, they feel themselves not getting the oxygen they need to function. They feel their consciousness slipping away and they feel the dizziness becoming overwhelming. These experiences reinforce the feelings of helplessness and lack of control. Unless someone intervenes and coaches them to slowly regain control of their breathing, they will pass out and potentially hurt themselves even worse.

This is our intervention chapter. We have worked so hard for our success. We have pushed for our accomplishments through what felt like impossible odds. We have sacrificed and we have celebrated. When Chapter 5 ended, we were throwing parties and keeping focused. People started believing in us and we were gaining new allies and now – SOMETHING HAS GONE TERRIBLY WRONG!

We don't understand what happened. Everything was functioning as it should. We were on top of our game. We've had challenges before and we overcame them. We've even seen problems in advance before they became problems – but this… THIS WE

---

1. hyperventilation. Dictionary.com. Dictionary.com Unabridged (v 1.1). Random House, Inc. http://dictionary.reference.com/browse/hyperventilation (accessed: March 5, 2008).

WEREN'T READY FOR. This was not in the plan nor did we see it coming. We thought this area of our life was covered. This wasn't a problem area but it is now and we feel completely helpless. We feel like we have loss control over something that was completely controlled. WHAT HAPPENED? WHAT WENT WRONG? WHY IS THIS HAPPENING? HOW DID WE GET HERE? WHAT DID I DO? CAN THIS BE REAL?

NO!!!! THIS CAN'T BE HAPPENING!

Yes my friend, this is happening. It's bad. It's ugly and it's real. It feels like our life is hyperventilating. We feel like we can't get the air we need to breathe deep. We feel we can't get enough fresh air to function the way we desire. And we feel like we're blacking out. It feels like our consciousness is slipping away. All of the points we've read in the other chapters, all of the lessons we picked up from the pages don't seem to work for us right now. We are overwhelmed and WE DON'T KNOW WHAT TO DO!!!

That's why this chapter is here. We will hit the reset button in our lives and press forward. No, this does not mean we will start over. YOU ALREADY HAVE A GOOD FOUNDATION! We'll just return to it and build some more. However, before we proceed, STOP, TAKE A DEEP BREATH AND SLOW DOWN. Because life is moving fast, it doesn't mean you have to. Yes, slowly inhale and exhale and feel yourself regain control of your thoughts and emotions. Yes my friend, calm down.

Good. Now let's get started…

LOSING PERSPECTIVE

When things go wrong, we tend to focus on what's wrong. We panic and we lose perspective. Because the bottom has fallen out from under us, we run scared. We scramble to recuperate. And if we're not careful, we'll allow the event to rob us of our momentum. We'll empower the event to stop us from fulfilling our goal because we simply lost perspective. Therefore, we'll discuss 3 reasons we so easily lose perspective and some adjustments we can make to reset ourselves.

- **The Event was Sudden**

    No matter how well we plan, there is very little we can do to control the suddenness of a matter. Things go wrong and sometimes they go wrong fast. We'd like to have time to address them but life doesn't always work that way. Life does come hard and fast. Sometimes so fast that before we can process what just happened, something else goes wrong as well. The suddenness of the matter has blindsided us. It happened under our radar and out of our line of sight. By time we knew there was an issue, the issue was a monster. Moreover, because the issue happens so suddenly, it forces us to respond differently. Our response time is forced to speed up tremendously. This is what's scary for us. If it was just the suddenness of the matter that was the problem, we could deal with it after its initial shock. However, it's not just the initial shock of the matter, but the matter is forcing us to address it in a timetable we're not used to. We can't go through our normal processing. We can't take our time evaluating the pros and cons. Decisions need to be made and they need to be made NOW. This is what terrifies us. We're becoming paralyzed and everything around us is falling apart! We're not moving fast enough! We're losing control!

    RESET:

    GET A GRIP!!! Yes, we are losing control! We're not losing control of the situation. We're losing control of ourselves. We're hyperventilating. We're too anxious. The situations are determining our feelings and not us. We have to slow down our feelings and make our thoughts coherent once again. You are not some helpless little girl running around clueless as to what to do. Be quiet. Be still. Reset yourself. What are you doing? You aren't some little boy who needs his momma to come wipe his nose because you've been "snot crying" about spilled milk. "Man up!" Slow your roll. Pump your brakes. Reset yourself. **Reality check: life will come fast at times and we'll deal with it when it does**. Whatever life has planned for us, there is a response for it (even if we don't have it). Never forget that. Regain control of yourself. Reclaim control of your thoughts. This is not the end. It's only the beginning. Strength comes through resistance. This is resistance. SO LET'S GET BUFF!!!

PERSPECTIVE ADJUSTMENTS:

In the immediacy of the moment, life and people can make us feel like we need to have the answers and we need to have them now. In some cases, that is true but not all. Sometimes we can take our time. We must never let the context control our decisions. We must make our decisions with clarity and self-control. One story capturing such a concept is the story about Jesus and his friend Lazarus.

> *"Now a certain man was sick, named Lazarus, of Bethany, the town of Mary and her sister Martha. Therefore his sisters sent unto him, saying, Lord, behold, he whom thou lovest is sick. When Jesus heard that, he said, This sickness is not unto death, but for the glory of God, that the Son of God might be glorified thereby. When he had heard therefore that he was sick, he abode two days still in the same place where he was. Then after that saith he to his disciples, Let us go into Judaea again. Then when Jesus came, he found that he had lain in the grave four days already. Then said Martha unto Jesus, Lord, if thou hadst been here, my brother had not died. Jesus saith unto her, Thy brother shall rise again. And when he thus had spoken, he cried with a loud voice, Lazarus, come forth. And he that*

was dead came forth, bound hand and foot with grave clothes: and his face was bound about with a napkin. Jesus saith unto them, Loose him, and let him go" (John 11: 1, 3-4, 6, 17, 21, 23, 43-44 King James Version).

Jesus took his time in making a decision when everyone around him wanted him to move now. Can you imagine what was running through people's minds when Jesus got the news that his dear friend was sick unto death and Jesus didn't move for 2 days? How would you feel if you were sick and you sent word to your friend to visit you because you knew they could make you feel better and they didn't move from their house for another 48 hrs? Most of us would have been hurt and angry. Some of us would've jumped to the conclusion the person we thought cared really didn't care. However, regardless of the opinion of others and the demand for immediate response, Jesus did not allow the context to make his decision for him. He made his decision for himself. He took his time. And the rest of the story follows that all ended well. We can take our time in making some decisions when the situation presses us to decide now but we must be in control of our emotions and thoughts. THIS IS A PERSPECTIVE ADJUSTMENT.

It is important I do bring some points of the story to light. First, it took a day or two to travel from where Jesus was to Lazarus' location (depending on the caravan and the conditions of travel). When Jesus and the posse arrived, Lazarus was already dead for 4 days. Since it took 1-2 days to travel (which practically speaking it was 2 days because Jesus was in no rush to begin with and he had 12 other men traveling with him by foot), it's safe to conclude that Lazarus was dead before Jesus even left. Which means if Jesus left immediately when he received the news, by time he would have arrived to Lazarus' location, Lazarus would have still been dead. My point is just because people make something sound urgent doesn't mean the outcome would change even if you jumped at it on the first word. If Jesus came immediately, Lazarus would have still died. Jesus did not come to stop Lazarus from dying. He came that God would receive acknowledgement. The context did not determine Jesus' agenda - Jesus determined it. Likewise my friend, don't allow the situation to determine your decision – YOU DETERMINE IT! THIS IS A PERSPECTIVE ADJUSTMENT.

Now there will be times when we do need to give immediate answers. We don't have time to sit down and figure out what are the pros and cons according to the way we've done it. We need to do all of that in a moment. And this is what frightens many of us. So the 1st thing we need to do is ACCEPT THAT THOSE TIMES ARE REAL AND THEY WILL COME. There is no getting around it. There's no reason to be afraid of it because those types of moments are inevitable. The sooner we accept it, the sooner we can move on. THIS IS A PERSPECTIVE ADJUSTMENT.

Secondly, when those moments come we need to SHUT UP AND LISTEN! Don't get it twisted about these types of scenarios. These are CRISIS moments. We don't have the time or the luxury of discovering who's the blame. We'll handle that later. Right now, we need to address the issue. We need the facts about the issue. We need the conditions affecting the issue. We need to know the parties impacting the issue. Once those details are gathered, we can give a time sensitive answer to a time sensitive dilemma. Yes, this process will move fast, hence, it's imperative we learn to shut up and listen. We must silence our thoughts and feelings in order to hear clearly the details of the issue. We cannot effectively listen to what is being said while we're trying to figure out who dropped the ball. If we do, then we'll miss vital information that would be key in constructing our solutions. We must remember: first things first. Placing blame is a secondary matter. It's not the most important in a crisis. This is why we must control ourselves. Discipline within ourselves is a must. It is non-negotiable. We must silence our thoughts so we can hear clearly. Listening is vital because the information is all around us and we must first have the information before we can create potential solutions. If we're talking, we're not listening. It's really just that simple. So be quiet and listen. When we speak, let it be a question to draw out more information (and not discover blame). Remember, discovering blame is a secondary focus. Keep your eyes on the prize. THIS IS A PERSPECTIVE ADJUSTMENT.

Finally, in crisis moments, we must DECIDE. We must make decisions. Setbacks will occur but we must address the issue with a solution. Others may think they should make the call but this decision is our decision to make and no one else's. Sometimes we don't have the answers at the time we would like to have them. THAT'S OK. We're built to be managers. None of us are built to be God. So let's leave the all-knowingness to God and let's focus on managing. I am the CEO of my own company and there are plenty of things I don't know. I can admit that but it doesn't dismiss my responsibility to manage the issue. So it becomes my responsibility to find the answer if I don't have the answer. All of us are in the same category. All of us are the CEOs of our lives. We make the final decisions directly affecting our lives. So make the call. This is our life. These are our dreams. We accept full responsibility for the outcomes. We will not shirk back from the task. We accept the responsibility of making the decision and so it follows we're making the decision. THIS IS A PERSPECTIVE ADJUSTMENT.

- **The Event has <u>Personal Significance</u>**

What went wrong affects us personally. Our projects are connected to our heart and soul. If our interactions were just some business deal, we could care less. However, it's not just some business deal. It's not some insignificant transaction we do on a daily basis. This is OUR LIFE! Yes, we're emotional when it comes to this. Yes, we'll become defensive and get sensitive about this. It's our feelings, our hopes, and our dreams on the line. And when we feel our dreams slipping through our fingers, fear grips us in ways no language can articulate. For some of us, we're afraid of failing. We're afraid of starting something we can't finish. And there's nothing more disappointing than to pursue your dreams and feel like your dreams are impossible to reach. When we are pursuing our heart's desire and something goes wrong, our soul hyperventilates. We can't get air out of our emotions. We can't get air out of our thoughts. Our ideas are scattered and life feels like its spinning out of control. We are so emotionally intertwined with our projects; we easily lose focus when things go wrong. When the project appears like it's going underwater, we interpret it to mean OUR LIVES ARE GOING UNDER WATER.

<u>RESET:</u>

Our lives are not going under water! It just means the road we're traveling either has ended (and we need to find the next road) or we have to modify our traveling arrangements. First things first; don't minimize your own strength! You have made it this far. Do you really believe you can't take anymore? Are you honestly convinced you can't handle another bad experience? Man, you better smack yourself back to reality! Girl, you better shake some sense into yourself! Making our dreams come to fruition is not easy. We are going to push in ways we didn't know we could push. We are reaching in places we didn't know we had strength. The reality is life is tough! Life is hard! Life is difficult and WE ARE BUILT FOR IT! We can take what life will throw at us, repackage it for our advantage and then we'll throw it back! You are no weakling. You are no punk. You are strength. You are destined for success. So stop acting like your world is falling apart. It's not. Yes, this is personal. Yes, this is significant. So stop crying about what didn't work. HIT THE RESET BUTTON AND LET'S FIND SOMETHING

THAT DOES WORK!

PERSPECTIVE ADJUSTMENTS:

I said earlier we need to find a new road because the old one we we're traveling have come to an end or we need to make some modifications. Let's explore the first option. My friend, some people will be with us for various seasons (some short and others long) and there will be others who will stay for a lifetime. Regardless of how long people will be in our lives, no one will be with us forever. Parents can walk with us for as long as they are here on earth and then there time is up. And there are other sad times whereby the child's time ends before the parents. Neither experience is pleasant. Neither experience is a desire but both are a certain reality. All of us will die. I hate to sound so cavalier about it but this is a truth we must accept; death is part of life. Just as all things are born, all things will die. Depending on your religious convictions death is viewed in many different ways but most religions acknowledge death as part of life. THIS IS A PERSPECTIVE ADJUSTMENT.

When I speak of death though, I'm not merely referring to the expiration of one's physical life. Death occurs in other ways. Marriages die. Friendships die. Careers die. All of these things we hold dear and precious to our hearts. For the one who wants to stay in the marriage, your heart is connected to that man or woman. And as much as we would like to believe that all of our praying, praising, and crying out to God will save our marriage, sometimes the marriage still ends in divorce. It doesn't mean God didn't hear you. It doesn't mean you didn't try hard enough. It does mean for whatever reason there are, the marriage has ended. I will not presume to have an answer as to why. The truth is I don't know. I would love to tell you why your marriage ended just so you could have closure, but I can't. That road has come to an end and you my friend, must move on. THIS IS A PERSPECTIVE ADJUSTMENT.

For the one who has lost his/her friend, it just doesn't seem right, does it? I know you've been friends for years. We've been through so much with our friends. They've seen us when we looked like a million dollars. They've seen us when we had bad breath, unshowered for days, funky, hair uncombed, food on the counter, and trash on the floor. We've been through arguments and fights, laughter and silly moments and now…it just doesn't seem fair. Who would have known pursuing our dreams would cause such havoc in friendships we thought we would have for a lifetime? Who would have known? Yet, pursuing our dreams did create this situation and now they have put us in a position to choose. Them or our dreams. It's not a fair ultimatum because we prefer to have both. If they can't live with both, then we will choose and they will lose. We have sacrificed too much at this point not to press on to see what the end will be for us. So those roads close as well. But for every road that comes to an end, there is always another road to travel, even if it means we pioneer the road ourselves. There will always be a road to travel regardless of what ends. THIS IS A PERSPECTIVE ADJUSTMENT.

Secondly, because something went wrong in our course, it doesn't mean our pursuit has come to end. It may mean we need to make some modifications. I was watching the National Treasurer starring John Cage and he said, "*Thomas Edison tried 2000 times to make a light bulb work. When someone asked him how did he press on after failing so many times, Edison replied, "I didn't fail. I found 2000 ways not to make light when I only need one to make it"*". Thomas Edison had a perspective adjustment. He refused to see his project as a failure but as an opportunity to modify. We cannot be afraid to look at what went wrong. In my personal life, I've discovered how not to do stuff because I screwed up so many times. I'm passionate about keeping my finances right because I've bounced plenty of checks and I had plenty of overdraft charges when I was younger. There is truth in stuff going wrong, if we're willing to look at it. However, the blessing of success is not merely looking at it, but making some changes and doing it again. When we can step back from our personal feelings, assess the situation for what it is, make changes, and try again, there will be nothing capable of stopping us. THIS IS A PERSPECTIVE ADJUSTMENT.

- **The Event was Negatively Labeled**

  When things go wrong, it's easy to go negative. The world sucks. Kids are bad. The wife is annoying. The husband is stupid. The boss is idiotic and so forth and so on. It's easy to spit venom. We curse out loved ones. We treat friends badly and we're not approachable. Negativity consumes us. We see the world as "hell on earth". Our ability to fairly judge situations becomes severely impaired because we've become incarcerated to negative attitudes. We're prisoners to our own pessimism. When we go negative with each response, we slowly creep away from the deep meaningful perspectives we developed in Chapter 1 and we slowly slide backwards to the shallow perspectives we had prior to reading this book. **Remember, perspectives develop out of consistent responses to various moments in life**. Perspectives are nothing more than habitual lenses through which we see life. Therefore, if we have a positive perspective, its only because we had consistent positive responses to good and bad experiences in life. And so the principle follows for a negative perspective. If we have a positive perspective (which you still do have) and we slowly start responding negatively, we're unintentionally forfeiting our productive perspective to adopt an unproductive one.

  When we go negative, we call experiences by the "**wrong**" name. I say, "wrong" because the name we assign to something is not the name we want it to be for us. If we call a situation "hopeless" it's not because we really believe it's hopeless. We're frustrated and our negativity is naming the situation. We are not naming it based on our desired outcome and therein lies our dilemma of losing perspective. **The problems with negatively labeling our experience are we consciously, subconsciously, and unconsciously treat them according to the name we give them.** If we name a situation "stupid", the action follows we don't take the matter seriously. What we name our experiences will position our perspective to see it as such motivating our actions to treat it as such. When we lose perspective, we lose productive actions because we have assigned the "wrong" names to our experiences. And once that occurs, our frustrations reinforce our pessimism compiling one "bad" experience (wrong name) on top of the other until we simply quit trying altogether. This is why we must recognize such negativity is a direct indication we're losing our positive perspective. We must hit our internal RESET BUTTON.

RESET:

IT'S JUST A SETBACK. It's not a failure. It's not the end of the world. It's just a setback. We must learn to STEP BACK with our SETBACKS. Step back and reassess the situation again. Step back and reconsider your options. Stepping back means we are able to move with our situations and re-adjust when something isn't working. SETBACKS ARE OUR OPPORTUNITIES TO STEP BACK AND REMODIFY OUR EFFORTS. Keep your positive expectations in front of your immediate attention. This will help guide our view of our situation. The glass is not half empty but half full. So what if milk spilled out. All it means is our glass is now 2/5ths full and not 3/5ths empty. Our goal is to be FULL NOT EMPTY. So there will never be a time where we are empty on any level because we aim, strive and labor forward to be full. DON'T FORGET THAT! We did not persevere this far to get an empty mentality now. Take a deep breath. Get a hold of yourself. Remember why you started this process. Remember why you wanted your life to be different. Look at this setback and decide what you want out of it. Give it the "right" name, a name invoking positive attitudes not negative thoughts. NOW LET'S RESET OURSELVES!

PERSPECTIVE ADJUSTMENTS:

Have you ever woke up out of a good sleep? Drowsy and exhausted, you realize you have an overwhelming urge to go to the restroom. It's not something you can hold off till the morning. You have a need to go to the restroom and you need to go now. So you roll over, placing your feet on the ground you make your way to the restroom. And then it happens. At 3 am in the morning, you stub your toe. If anyone could see you in that moment, his or her opinion of you would completely change. Jumping up and down, cursing and swearing, kicking the wall or chair as if it walked into us, the irony to the story is our bodies are not in total pain but simply - our toe. Quite often, we lose focus when we experience pain and act as if the pain is all consuming when it's only in a small section of our lives. Keep the pain in perspective. This is not "hell on earth"! Stop labeling the world as problematic when it's just an issue. Control your emotions. Keep them within their context. It's foolishness to allow our emotions to run without restraint. So restrain them. I'm an advocate for being in touch with our emotions, but I refuse to advocate emotions controlling our decisions. Name your experiences **with** your emotions but don't be dictated **by** them. We must adjust our feelings and ourselves. Otherwise passion without restraint will make us reckless to others and ourselves. THIS IS A PERSPECTIVE ADJUSTMENT.

Losing perspective is a dangerous reality for us. It's dangerous because we can abandon everything we worked so hard to achieve in a short amount of time. With unproductive outlooks to life and people, we can unknowingly sabotage our own desires while thinking it's truly someone else's fault. We run the risk of becoming self-deluded in our thinking and impotent to make change. This is potential reality we face when we lose perspective. And in case some of us have already begun losing perspective, hit the reset button and make some perspective adjustments.

STOP!

BREATHE DEEP! & CONSIDER!

1. Think of an event where something went wrong quickly. How did you respond to it? Why?

2. Think of an event where something was personally significant to you and it went horribly wrong. How did you respond to it? Why that response?

3. What names are you calling your setbacks? Are the names you're giving your setbacks invoking positive/negative attitudes? What are the actions proceeding after your naming the setback? Are they productive or destructive? Why?

4. How have you consistently seen your problems? Why?

5. What do your setbacks put you in remembrance of? Why is that situation so vital to how you see life now?

REMEMBERING YOUR PLATFORM

One of my favorite past times is watching movies. Going to the theatre is great and all, but getting a good movie you've never seen, ordering some pizza, nachos with spicy salsa, homemade spaghetti with the buttered rolls that melt in your mouth (and not in your hand), drinking some good old fashioned purple or red Kool-Aid with sweet potato pie on the side is simply - the BEST!!! As you can see movies at my house are ridiculously fulfilling. I could go on and on about that, but I really enjoy watching movies, especially action packed martial art films with a decent story line (if there is such a thing). However, of all the parts in those types of movies, I like the part where the fighter loses his way and finds his way back to what he/she was taught in earlier years. Those parts of the movie resonate strongly with me because I have so many times lost my way and had to find it again. In the movies, the fighter usually has to fight through incredible odds to achieve what he/she set out to do. However, something went horribly wrong and they didn't see it coming. Usually the experience is so tragic that it threatens their status in a competition or even their continued existence altogether. They lose themselves in the setback and hence they become careless and reckless. As the movie proceeds, someone of significance (either from the past or present) coaches them (if only in spirit) back to where they should be. And the first 2 paths the fighter travels is the path of facing his/herself and the path of remembering the lessons of old.

This is what this section is for. My friend, just like the movies, we are fighters as well. We have to fight through impossible odds to achieve our goals and dreams. We experience success and we encounter setbacks. However, there are some setbacks striking us at our core. It hurts. It hurts us so bad we become careless and reckless. We get negative. We act out of anger and rage. We're fearful and we lose our way. We no longer fight our enemies but we abuse our friends. We attack our loved ones. We disregard our spouses. We're insensitive to our children. WE HAVE BECOME THE ENEMY WE SWORE WE WOULD FIGHT! And now, we need to make our way back to being the man or woman we said and know we need to be. We must once again fight. This fight is not a fight against flesh and blood. It's a fight to remember. It's fight to recall why we chose to fight in the first place. This is our fight and no one else can fight it for us. My friend let us fight! LET US…REMEMBER!

- **CHANGE**

    Why are you reading this book? Why did you select this book

from others? Why are you considering the questions I ask you throughout chapters? Why are you writing your answers at the end? You're not reading this book just because you like to read. You're not reading this book just because you have nothing to do. And as handsome as I would like to think I am, you're not reading this book because I'm on the front cover. The truth is you're reading this book because you want CHANGE! You're looking at your life and you don't like what you see. You don't like what you feel. There are things and experiences you don't want anymore. There are people you need to change your interaction with. Your desire for change keeps you engrossed in the words on the page and connects you to my spirit as I write to you. You feel me and I feel you. I hear you saying, "*There's got to be something different than this. Better than this*". And there is something different and better than what you're experiencing.

However, change will not happen osmosisly. Change begins with us. The change we want must first, be the change we are. We must become that which we desire to see. In tragedies, we must remain the change agent. In setbacks, we must step back and remember we're the change agents. When people tell us we haven't changed, we must continue to be change. Otherwise, there can be no change for the better, not for us. If we want change, we must accept the responsibility and privilege of being the change for others to see, even if and when they don't see it. We must still be the change. Yes, we want change. So yes, we must change our perspectives, our motives, our expectations, and our actions. We must focus our efforts on changing ourselves and our environment surrounding us WILL change. For us, we must remember BREATHING DEEP MEANS CHANGE. We cannot forget what that means or we will lose our way. Remember, you started this journey for change. You built this platform for change. Therefore, don't stop laboring until you have the change you desire. REMEMBER YOUR PLATFORM.

- **ABUNDANCE**

    We started this journey because we're tired of barely having enough. Some days we don't even have that. We're tired of seeing people prosper by illegal means and we struggle legally. People get over and we pay taxes. People live large and are destructive while we try to make a dollar out fifteen cents and volunteer our time with the Boy Scouts. WE WANT MORE. We're tired of living paycheck to paycheck. We tired of going to Check-N-Cash because we don't have enough money to pay our bills to only perpetuate the cycle again the following week when we get paid. We want to live in prosperity and abundance. And it's not limited to just our finances but we want abundance in healthy relationships, emotional peace, mental clarity, spiritual communion, physical health, environmental safety, and sexual satisfaction. We want to live in a place of MORE THAN ENOUGH. We're tired of borrowing. We want to be the lender. We tired of asking for help. We want to help ourselves and bless others. We're tired of asking for a ride. It's time we bless someone with a car debt-free (and still have our own car to drive debt-free).

    For many of us, BREATHING DEEP MEANS LIVING IN A PLACE OF ABUNDANCE. That's why you're reading this book. Therefore, it behooves us to adopt an abundant attitude now, though we're currently broke. This is not wishful thinking because we are doing much more than thinking. WE'RE CREATING! We're creating the abundant life we want for our families, friends and ourselves. Before we do anything, we will remember – FIRST. We're remembering why we started this journey. We're remembering the results we experienced when we applied what we read to our lives. We're remembering the answers to the questions we discovered about ourselves. We're remembering not to allow the context to change our perspective, not to allow life to deter us from our dreams, and not to allow people's opinion to poison our pursuit. We will remember our own abundance. We are full of productive ideas. We are full of successful abilities. Despite our setbacks, we are full of confidence. Yes my friend, we are full of abundance. We have healthy relationships because *we* are in the relationship. We have safe neighborhoods because *we* live there. And yes, we have awesome, spectacular, and mind-blowing sex lives because *we* are making love. Never allow your setbacks to steal your memory. Fight to remember. Remember the value of your own abundance. Remember your need for abundance. Remember your labor to abundance. REMEMBER YOUR PLATFORM!

- **MEANING**

All of us need our lives to mean something. I believe none of us can truly live life if we believed it counted for nothing. For this reason so many people commit suicide. Some of them believe their lives are worthless and insignificant. I know because I use to be one of those people. Like others, I wanted to kill myself and was almost successful until someone showed me that others did value me taught me how to truly value myself. He taught me I had meaning and significance. He showed me how to see others. I learned that people did affirm me. I really was valuable to others. And as I learned to see myself as full of meaning and significance, I attracted people that treated me accordingly. Some people misdiagnose my confidence but that's ok too. I know who I am and to this day I'm that man who remembers his significance. You have meaning and significance as well. You're weary of men minimizing your contributions. Women only seeing your benefits and never affirming your worth frustrate you. You're annoyed by companies employing you as a token when you know you've worked three times harder for only one-third the credit. You need life to mean something more than what it's meant.

If you're like me, you have asked yourself plenty of times, "*What am I worth to people? What is my life worth? Will anyone miss me when I'm gone*". These questions don't mean we're psychologically confused. These questions don't mean we struggle with low self-esteem. They do mean we have questions of our significance to others and ourselves and no one is exempt from such affirmation. We all need it. We need positive affirmation of our significance in relationships, in our careers, and in our marriages. And as sad of a reality as it may be, if we don't get the affirmation we need to feel safe, secure, and stable in our relationships, we'll eventually venture somewhere else to find it. For such a reason, infidelity occurs. This is not an excuse for infidelity but it is a reason. While there are many other reasons why people cheat, I speak only of this reason – affirmation of our worth. Yes, all of us can affirm ourselves but we need others to affirm us too. That's why we join fraternities and sororities, social clubs, attend church, have friends and more. We need others to affirm us. We need other people to value us and we need people we can value.

We get in intimate relationships not just for the company of someone else but we want to love someone. We have a need to affirm people. We have needed to show people how special they are to us. Some of us do it really well. Some of us don't but all of us have our own way of affirming loved ones and friends. That's one of the reasons why infidelity hurts so deeply. It hurt so deeply because we gave our own soul as **the** measuring standard of our love for the other person and to cheat, it feels like our affirmation of their worth was not enough for them. How does one deal with their soul not being enough? How does we reconcile within ourselves our hearts were not enough affirmation? There are no words to capture the pain of such rejection. There is no groan uttered in the pages of time in this universe or any other capable of articulating accurately - our pain. The need for meaning, significance and worth drives many of us.

And for many of us, BREATHING DEEP MEANS HAVING A LIFE WORTH SOMETHING! This book is in your hands right now because you need your life to count. I desire the same for you for it is the same desire I had for myself. We desire a life we can be proud of. We desire a life meaningful and not shallow. We want our experiences to count for something. **Our lives must count for more than catalogue of memories!** Therefore, let us remember our own worth. Let us remember the value of who we truly are. Let us remember our hard times and how we made it. Let us remember the love we still have regardless of how many times ungrateful people tried to choke out our compassion. We still have it! We still haven't abandoned our confidence in marriage though we're divorced. Remember that. We've not aborted I desires to be happy with a spouse though our relationships have been crappy. Remember that. We still believe there's someone who'll love us for us and not try to change us. Remember that. My friend, remember! Remember you are a good woman. Remember you are a good man. Remember you are a good parent. Remember you will make someone proud to be your mate. Remember you'll create beautiful moments and blessed memories. Remember people will learn from your life. Youth will sit in your company to hear the words you speak. Yes, meaning and significance was why you started this trip. And though there have been some setbacks, those setbacks are powerless to set back your worth. You built this platform for a life a new meaning. You dug this platform's foundation of worth. And now I encourage you in a time where setbacks try to steal our thunder – REMEMBER YOUR PLATFORM.

STOP!

BREATHE DEEP! & CONSIDER!

1. Do you remember why you started this journey? What is it?

2. Will you allow life's experiences or people to rob you of your reasons for starting this journey? Why not?

3. Will you use your memory of success over adversity to fuel your drive to finish what you started? Why?

4. <u>Will you finish what you started? Why?</u>

Our platforms are huge to our success. They are the principles, motives, and reasons why we do anything. To forget our platforms is suicide in itself. And while none of us willing say to ourselves, "*hey, let's forget why we're doing this*" life happens in such a way that we do forget why we started. We become so overwhelmed by the setback, we focus on the setback, we mislabel the setback that we forget the setback is really nothing more than – just a setback. We forget the setback is happening within a larger scope. We focus so much on what went wrong with the setback that we fail to step back and see what went right.

One of the other steps we need to take in remembering our platform is remembering our inventory. In Chapter 1, we spent a considerable amount of time assessing our toolbox. Therefore, it's only wise that we quickly revisit our tools and how they can help us move forward towards the fulfillment of our dreams.

- **<u>YOUR DREAMS</u>**

We discussed that your dreams have a two-fold affect in our lives. First, they give us direction. Our dreams are the places where we want to live. They're the type of lifestyles was want to have. They're the types of relationships we desire for ourselves. Secondly, our dreams give us a present standard for living. If we want to be a good spouse tomorrow, we need to conduct ourselves in the same manner today. Otherwise, we will not be what we dream to be, but we will remain as we are. Marriage is not magic. People don't get married and magically blossom into something new. Newness in marriage takes work. There are no short cuts. If anything happens in marriage naturally without effort, it would be marriage brings out the stuff you didn't see through the dating and the engagement.

Now pertaining to using your dreams to push through setbacks, our dreams are what we **don't** have. They are the stuff we're working towards. They are the trophies at the end of the race. They are the finish line. Our setbacks are what we **do** have. So ask yourself the question, "*Which one did I start this race for – the setbacks or the dreams*". If you're honest with yourself, you'll answer with your dreams. So use your dreams as the motivation to keep pressing. You did not run this race without including the fact there would be some setbacks. You knew these days were coming and now they're here. So since they have come, let them go and press onward to dreams. Our dreams are there for us to continually look at. They guide our course. As long as we can see our dreams, we are on the right road. Did hear what I just said? AS LONG AS YOU CAN SEE YOU DREAMS YOU ARE ON THE RIGHT ROAD! That means even if you've had a setback, if you can see your dreams, then you're still in a good place. Setbacks mean you moved back. They don't mean you're off course. So adjust and modify and move forward again.

- **YOUR STRENGTHS**

This is where our confidence builder is. We have gone through difficult times in our lives. Plenty of them were so bad we felt we'd never overcome them. Yet we did. Our strengths were forged in the heat of adversity. In short, we got better the tougher times got. Do you think this is any different? Do you think your skills won't sharpen this time around? I've said this before and I'll reiterate again here: You're built for this. You can take this and throw it back. So throw it back and move on!

- **YOUR WEAKNESSES**

This is where your team comes in. Setbacks tend to make us feel insufficient. Setbacks make us feel like we can't do it alone. And in that case, the setback is correct in making us feel that way. We are not a one-man show. We need help. That's probably why the setback happened in the first place. Some of us were too stubborn to take heed in Chapter 1, so we're doing damage control in Chapter 6. Some of us are so full of pride thinking we know everything that we make careless mistakes simply because we won't listen. Here's a reality check, my friend. YOU DON'T KNOW EVERYTHING! I had to learn that lesson. You're not the exception. Get it in your head. Internalize the concept. You need other people. You don't have all the answers. Let other people give you what you don't have. Let other people help you where you can't help yourself. Let other people do what they do best while you do what you do best. Lay down your pride. Put your ego off to the side. **Your weaknesses are invitations for others to invest in your dreams.** So let them invest! Nobody can ally with you or support you if you act as if you don't need their help. You are getting in the way of your own success because you are too naive to realize there are people who believe in you just as much as you believe in yourself. Hush your pride and let people bless you.

- **YOUR FAITH**

    This is where our peace and a good night's sleep are. Let's face it; there are things that are out of our control. We don't like what those things are. And in most cases we never really know what those things are until we start working on it only to discover our effort is not making a difference. For many of us, we have a hard time facing this simple truth. WE CANNOT CONTROL EVERYTHING. So let's let our faith do what we can't. We can't control it but our faith says the setback is controllable. So let's believe it and move on.

    Now of course, there are those of who know what faith says in theory but we don't believe it practically. For some of us, it's simple. We don't believe it because we don't like it. We don't like being out of control. We don't like the fact there is a possibility we can plan every item, know every detail and still have something go horribly wrong. However, arguing that point is futile. There are things we can't control. That's the bottom line. SO GET OVER IT! None of us like being in a situation we can't control. However, it happens. The sooner we accept life is not 100% controlled by us, the sooner we can major in the majors and minors in the minors. The longer it takes for us to accept this point, the more time we'll waste and the more energy we'll exert on matters we need not be bothered with. We empower setbacks to rob our faith because we choose to believe we can control everything. So let's rest and relax and let our faith give us the assurance that all is well with our soul. Besides, the only people who should worry about such matters are those who choose to not have faith in their toolbox. Those people have a right to worry because those people believe they can control 100% of what happens to them. Eventually, they'll come to the place I'm speaking of. One day, they will certainly come this place.

STOP!

BREATHE DEEP! & CONSIDER!

1. Can you still see your dreams after the setback?

2. Will you let people help you? How do you plan to do that?

3. Do you still have faith? How do you know?

4. Are you practicing faith in uncontrollable situations? How so?

TEAM EFFORT

In Chapter 2 we discussed having a team. When setbacks happen, this is when you call your team together. My personal conviction is "United we stand, divided is not an option". In other words, if my success is our success, then my setback is our setback as well". From personal experience, when things go wrong is when we see real teammates and jersey wearers. Real teammates get in the mud to make our goal a success. Jersey wearers want the glory without the sacrifice. They are the pretty boys who run their trap but lack action. They're the 1st to run on stage and be in the spotlight and always the last to roll up their sleeves and get dirty. Avoid the jersey wearers. They're leaches riding off of our blood, sweat, and tears while they themselves never break a sweat. Kick them off your team.

We need teammates bearing down in the forth quarter while all of us are tired and exhausted. We need teammates who understand the meaning of going the extra mile. Real teammates understand when they need to come over our house as we break down and cry. They know when we need to get out of the house. They can handle us venting and rambling as we get issues of our chest. Real teammates can handle our issues and us. Yes, we have issues and our teammates know what they are and they still refrain from judging us. We disagree with teammates, fight with teammates, but they never quit the team. Loyalty is a rarity. And when we find people who are loyal, we embrace them and celebrate them but we never abuse them.

When it comes to overcoming our setbacks, it will be a team effort as well. Yes, we have our part to do as individuals but we also have parts to do as a team. However my friend, this is where trust comes to be a factor. You are the lead to your team. Everyone is taking his or her lead off of you. So it must be understood the climate you set will be the climate everyone else will reinforce. In order to give our team the opportunity to come through for us, we must call a timeout and say we need help. We must become vulnerable. Just because people are on our teams doesn't mean they can read our minds. They don't know our crankiness means we're stressed. They don't know our silence means we're angry. They don't know our sarcasm means something has offended us. Remember, they're teammates, not God. They are not all knowing. So we must stop treating them as if they are. WE MUST SAY SOMETHING!

Our team believes in us. They believe we're winners. They believe we can achieve our dreams and reach our goals. And it must equally follow that we display the same confidence in them as they do in us. We must believe in them. We must tell them they are winners. We must empower the people who follow us to lead themselves. This is the time where they can take the lead for a while. So let's let them lead. While I was consulting a ministry about the leadership of the ministers, the pastor would never let the associate ministers do anything. He was burnt out and his delivery was the equivalent of eating a Big Mac value meal microwaved after being in the refrigerator (and you know how McDonald's fries taste when they get cold). It was horrible. I asked him, *"What is the point in having the ministers on staff if they're simply there to look important"*. He said, *"They weren't ready for leadership"*. I said, *"How are they suppose to get ready if you won't let them do anything. Let them lead for a moment. Give them the opportunity to show you what they got. You may be pleasantly surprised"*. Needless to say my advice was turned down and slowly he started losing members. We must let our team take the lead from time to time. We must let them make mistakes so they can learn as we're learning ourselves. If it's true that we are a team, then all of us will make mistakes and all of us can learn from each other.

That's the beauty of a team. None of us are alone. We have each other.

STOP!

BREATHE DEEP! & CONSIDER!

1. Do you trust your teammates? How do you know?

2. Do you have more teammates than jersey wearers? How do you plan to keep them or make adjustments?

3. Have you told your teammates you need help or do you expect them to know you need help without your help? Why?

Chapter 6
Pressing Onward

Setbacks are difficult places to maneuver. So much is at risk when we have those types of experiences. Yet, there is so much help as well. We've discussed much in this chapter. Take some time to further empower yourself. Answering these questions will give you a greater sense of security in knowing you're not crazy or senile. You are on track and you have what tit takes to endure and succeed. So stop, take a deep breath, overcome your setbacks, and press onward.

1. Think of an event where something went wrong quickly. How did you respond to it? Why?

2. Think of an event where something was personally significant to you and it went horribly wrong. How did you respond to it? Why that response?

3. What names are you calling your setbacks? Are the names you're giving your setbacks invoking positive/negative attitudes? What are the actions proceeding after your naming the setback? Are they productive or destructive? Why?

4. How have you consistently seen your problems? Why?

5. What do your setbacks put you in remembrance of? Why is that situation so vital to how you see life now?

6. Do you remember why you started this journey? What is it?

7. Will you allow life's experiences or people to rob you of your reasons for starting this journey? Why not?

8. Will you use your memory of success over adversity to fuel your drive to finish what you started? Why?

9. Will you finish what you started? Why?

10. Can you still see your dreams after the setback?

11. Will you let people help you? How do you plan to do that?

12. Do you still have faith? How do you know?

13. Are you practicing faith in uncontrollable situations? How so?

14. Do you trust your teammates? How do you know?

15. Do you have more teammates than jersey wearers? How do you plan to keep them or make adjustments?

16. Have you told your teammates you need help or do you expect them to know you need help without your help? Why?

CHAPTER 7

HAVEN'T SEEN YOU IN MINUTE
(Fire From Past Flames)

*"Stand fast therefore in the liberty wherewith Christ hath made us free, and be not **entangled** again with the yoke of bondage"*
(Galatians 5:1 King James Version)

"Asthma is a chronic disease that affects your airways. The airways are the tubes that carry air in and out of your lungs. If you have asthma, the inside walls of your airways are inflamed. The inflammation makes the airways very sensitive, and they tend to react strongly to things that you are allergic to or find irritating. When the airways react, they get narrower, and less air flows through to your lung tissue. This causes symptoms like wheezing (a whistling sound when you breathe), coughing, chest tightness, and trouble breathing, especially at night and in the early morning.[1]*"* Of the many ways to treat asthma, one of the most preferred recommendations is avoid trigger situations which prompt an asthma attack. In other words, stay away from things you know that aggravate your breathing.

Some of our intimate relationships felt just like Asthma attacks. One moment we're breathing normally and the next we're gasping for air. One moment we're cuddly and laughing and the next moment we're at each other's throat. We're hollering and screaming. We're getting mad, throwing tantrums, and losing our dignity. Asthma attacks are never pretty scenes and when we lose our cool, it's not pretty either. Even in a mild asthma attack, the person experiences a level of discomfort whereby it shows, if but to the person who knows him/her well enough to know there's a problem. However, one thing is certain; if a person continues to ignore the triggers of his/her asthma, that person will find themselves in a potentially dangerous and life threatening dilemma. And some of us have been that way in our relationships too. We've ignored some of those triggers and our lives, our finances, and even our peace of mind was placed in a potentially dangerous and life threatening dilemma. So we ended those relationships and vowed to ourselves to never find ourselves in those situations again. And for the most part, we never anticipated reneging on our promise, entering into a familiar situation, or entertaining a familiar past lover – UNTIL NOW.

This chapter is a unique chapter. It's unique because we'll exclusively deal with something very specific to all of our lives – intimate relationships. These types of relationships can make or break us. Yet there is something we need to be mindful of as we pursue this journey of making our dreams come true and achieving our goals. We must beware of past lovers creeping into our present lives. While there are some cases where past lovers reunited and life was great. There are other cases past lovers reunited and chaos worse than before occurred. Which one is our situation? Who knows.

However what makes a significant difference is the **timing** of everything. My friend, timing can be the difference between winning or losing, marriage or remaining single, a job or unemployment, and life or death. Timing is huge. Therefore, we will look at how a certain type of intimate relationship (namely past intimate relationships) and the timing thereof can cause us to have relational asthma attacks resulting in shallow breathing which takes us away from optimal performance in our everyday lives. We'll carefully come through how we met up, talked on the phone, and spent time in each other presence and the reality we'll have to soon come face-to-face with. Moreover, we'll draw out some clear reasons why sex is such an important topic to discuss and distinguishing the difference between making love to a person versus making love to the idea of a person.

Let's take a walk through this chapter looking at some experiences we've may overlooked from a different perspective. We may read something surprising or we may identify something helping us know our next course of action.

Let's begin...

THE CONTEXT

I think it's safe enough to say you and I believe setbacks can be a dangerous place to be. So many things can and will go wrong during setbacks. Our attitudes can change. Our behavior can become destructive and our perspective can shift. We can even lose focus on what's important. And one of the ways we know we have lost our way is **we get cold.** One of the first signs of getting cold is we become isolated. We disconnect from people. We stop talking. We go into a shell. We detach. Setbacks can make us feel unworthy and in response to feeling unworthy, we behave like we're unworthy. We don't hang out with friends. We won't spend time with family and we won't use our team. Though there was an entire section dedicated to the significance of having a team and letting them help us, many of us still choose to take the burden of the setback on ourselves. And in most cases, our spirits buckle under such unnecessary pressure. There are others of us who know the significance of our teams. We know the prayer partners we can call. We know our friends we can vent to and cry on and we still avoid them. Hence, we only make ourselves all the more isolated and we grow even colder.

Secondly, our rationale is indicating we've lost our way. We don't want to talk to our allies and teammates because talking to them is a reminder of a situation we don't want to acknowledge yet. We don't want to acknowledge there's a problem. We need to address issues but we choose to escape. We don't want to accept there's something that's gone terribly wrong. And every time we talk to our team, it's a very clear reminder there's business we need to handle and the truth is we want to forget it. We don't want to deal with the disappointment of the setback. We feel it's hard to deal with the difficulty and complexity of the matter. WE DON'T WANT TO BE BOTHERED WITH IT!

So we run. We run from our help. We run from our support. We duck and dodge our network. We don't want to feel their embrace. We don't want to hear their advice. We avoid their phone calls. We dismiss their encouragement. We delete their emails and we ignore their text messages. We make ourselves like Casper, the friendly ghost, and we politely, pleasantly, and silently disappear into the shadows of life. We withdraw. And we get even colder.

And simultaneously, we crave the heat of company, the kind of company stimulating romance and tender affection. We want the fire of affection. We want the kind of affection warming our souls and igniting our passions from the winter of isolation and loneliness (the isolation we brought on ourselves by running from our problems). We need heat. We crave fire. We want a body next to us, a person to be close to and connect with us in ways only groans, moans, and sighs of such pleasure can capture and articulate. Romantic intimacy, the kind of connection we need to affirm us personally providing us the romantic significance we desire. We don't have that kind of intimacy and hence we are even colder. We've alienated ourselves from our allies. They remind us of our setbacks. Besides, we don't connect with our allies like that. Our friends are our friends. We may kiss them but we don't **kiss** them. We may hug them but we don't **hug** them. We may even spend the night over their houses but we don't **sleep** with them. Do you get my point? We want someone who's not connected to our setbacks. We want our significant person's existence to be beyond the scope of what went wrong. We crave someone we can be close to without having to divulge our disappointments (of which we have yet to truly come to grips with). We're lonely. We're frustrated and we're cold. We don't want to deal with our setbacks because we **blame** our setbacks for putting us in a cold place.

We demand intimate connection and we demand it now. Our patience is dissipating. We need warmth now. We need affection now. We want to talk to someone whose company doesn't remind us of what we need to do. We want an escape. We need an outlet. We want to getaway and we want to do it with someone of significance now. We pant for these desires all the more than usual because we have cut ourselves off from people who love and support us. We don't realize we still need connections and if we abandon the connections of trust, we leave ourselves open to find intimate connections by another means. We abandon what we do know for something we don't. We've detached from our friends and we've limited our outlets. We constantly have issues building but we have no one to share them with. Our own decisions have cornered us against the wall and now we demand release. Desiring to be with someone intimately is natural. However, with no one to spring board our issues off of, the need for intimate connection becomes the substitute for meaningful relationships and the context of this situation already is built with a faulty and unstable foundation. In the meanwhile, we're getting cold and we option for the heat of intimacy to warm us up AND WE WANT IT NOW!!!

STOP!

BREATHE DEEP! & CONSIDER!

1. Have you isolated yourself because of how your setback made you feel? Why?

2. Have you blamed your setback for where you currently are in your life? Why?

3. Have you been looking for romance to substitute your team and validate your escape? Why?

THE ENCOUNTER

In most cases, we're usually minding our business when we run across someone from our romantic past. We didn't look them up (though the thought of calling them may have crossed our mind if we could remember them). We could have been working at a coffee shop, visiting a church, sitting in a meeting, accompanying a friend, or even on vacation when we see that man or woman we use to share so much with. At first, the encounter doesn't feel like it's happening. It seems unreal and it feels like a dream. We do second takes to make sure we are seeing what we think we're seeing. On the flip side, they may catch us completely off guard because we were there for a different purpose. They saw us and approached us. We were clueless they anywhere remotely in the vicinity. The initial reunion is unquestionably without reservation – a surprise.

Then the conversation begins. Still feeling awkward, they ask us the opening question "*Hey, how are you? I haven't seen you in awhile*". Still in awe, we usually answer something like, "*I'm doing well and yourself*". We're still trying to compose ourselves because this is not some random person we just met. This is someone of history, a particular history. We want to be pleasant because we are in public and we really don't want anyone knowing our business. Our personal lives is something we want to keep personal and this person in front of us at one point, used to be the most personally significant relationship we use to know. This is not information we want as a conversation topic. As much as possible, we try to keep it light and friendly. Some of us may even try to speak in a manner that suggestively sounds like we actually don't know them. Yes, it's a deceptive tactic and quite misleading. And our opinion is in a setting where people are always trying to find out more than they should, it's a tactic that keeps people minding their own business.

Usually, the initial conversation is light and short (unless the circumstances change). We have no need to panic because the interaction isn't long enough to panic. However, the second conversation in our encounter with them takes a different shift. Still in a public setting, we talk. Of course, the conversation doesn't start with "do you have a boyfriend or girlfriend" (and for those conversations that do, a clear message is being conveyed). The conversation does hone in on the person. Our past romantic interest takes an interest in how we are personally and how has our career been moving. Career advancement and business related conversations are always safe topics to start with little to know resistance. And we answer and we send back the same types of questions. Every now and then, a romantic personal question tries sliding in and in most cases, we're sharp enough in the situation whereby we shut it down and keep the conversation moving. They respect us and it's a refreshing notion for us to have a light conversation about the things we want to discuss and side step the topics we don't. Remembering our context, we don't want to talk about the setback (the topic we need to face head on) but we do want to talk about other stuff that makes us feel good. Though someone from our romantic past has come back into our lives (if but for a brief moment), it felt good to have a light and pleasant conversation with no pressure and no strings attached. As brief of an interaction as it may have been, for the first time in quite some time, we felt WARMTH!

    Feeling warmth is important to us because the whole purpose behind conversation is to connect. Whether the conversation exchanges information, ideas, opinions, current events, or whatever, connections undoubtedly occur. Since we have detached from our team, attaching to someone else by way of conversation is a must. We want to censor the flow of information about ourselves and with our team we can't do that but with strangers we can. So meeting a past romance is ok with us because we can say however much or little and they have to accept it. But here's where we begin feeling the impact of our detachment. Our past romance enjoyed the conversational exchange (and we did too) and he/she would like to continue contact without loosing touch like before. Promises of not revisiting the past and commitments to keeping the interaction pleasant and uneventful are all likely to be made as prerequisites to continued interaction. When an agreement is reached, the contact information is exchanged. We get their emails and phone numbers and vice versa. And while they are going their way and we are going ours, we feel a spark within because now we can connect how we want to connect. We feel empowered and we feel like we're making the rules. We feel we're regaining our sense of control (the same sense of control we felt was stolen from us by our setback). We feel strong again and WE FEEL HEAT!

STOP!

BREATHE DEEP! & CONSIDER!

1. How did you initially feel when you reconnected with a past romance? Why?

2. What was your context during the time you met your past romance? How did that affect your interaction with him/her?

3. Was the conversation refreshing? Why or why not?

4. Did you exchange contact information with them? Why?

5. What do you expect to happen between you and your past romance? Why?

THE PHONE CALLS

Phone calls can be delightful experiences or frustrating encounters. For instance, having telemarketers call us for any and everything is just annoying. Now we all know they each have a job to do and no one can blame them for doing their job. However, when we are the person having our house phone ring every hour on the hour (sometimes twice an hour), some of us tend to lose our patience with telemarketers. And there are some of us that just go irate after our personal telemarketing phone call threshold has been crossed. On the other hand, receiving that unexpected phone call from a friend from oversees or a friend who we haven't heard from in years is simply exciting. We can stay on the phone with them for hours catching up and learning all about their life and telling them about ours. Phone calls can be a bittersweet experience depending on who's on the other line.

In the same sense, phone calls extend our ability to connect. We remember the days when we were in high school. We would be on the phone for hours at a time. I remember plenty of times I was impatient with my parents because their business calls were tying up the line. I had girls I needed to call and my parents were just taking their good, old, sweet time. They were killing me. I also remember getting in trouble because I told my parents' friends my parents weren't home just so I could stay on the phone and talk to cheerleaders. Talking on the phone was significant to me because it connected me to people I couldn't be connected to. I had friends across the country and I could laugh with them in real time while letters took days to deliver. Many of us are the same way. We look forward to hearing our friends' voices via the phone. We can tell when they're excited and when something's wrong. We know if they're busy or if they've just awakened. When we can't see people face-to-face, our secondary form of contact is the phone. So when it comes to speaking on the phone, our ability to connect may not be as great as a face-to-face interaction, but phone calls are still significantly meaningful.

And just like our initial shock of surprise when we reconnected with our past romance in person, we experience something similar when they actually call us. We're surprised they call. Usually, they know we're surprised and they joke with us saying something like, "*You must have really believed I wasn't calling you*". The shock of the moment and the joke about it becomes a nice icebreaker to again make the conversation light and disarming. We allow them to take the lead in the conversation since they initiated the call. Again we hear the words, "*So tell me how are you because I haven't seen you in awhile*". We then engage them in conversations about our careers and general experiences with little personal inserts here and there. Except this time around, the conversation is a little more forthcoming and equally coy. The questions can be more forthcoming because the person asking doesn't have to see the person's reaction and hearing their reactions are easier to manage than looking at them. So they can be more direct. Secondly, the questions are coy because you don't see the person, which means you can say something and leave it open for interpretation. If we catch what they say and are offended, they can re-shift. If we catch what they say and don't comment, they move on. With all of this in light, we continue to censor our conversation. We are careful to not say something we don't want to discuss and we stay away from topics that could potentially spark unwelcomed inquiries. If in fact, they do ask an unwelcomed question, we can simply say we don't want to discuss it and move on. In doing this, our sense of control is slowly being restored all the more.

Our sense of control is not the only thing we're acquiring. We are also connecting and hence, we are generating heat. Let's get brutally honest here: this is what we want. We want to talk to someone on our own terms. We want to control how we develop our relationship because our ego was bruised because we couldn't control our setback. Therefore, rather than to deal with the problem, we believe we can create a parallel reality whereby the first reality will cease to exist on its own. Don't forget, we've allowed our setback to place us in a cold place. We've detached from our allies. We limit our conversations with our teammates. And so it follows, we are alone in a cold, disconnected, environment. Consequently, we are using this conversation as an opportunity to generate the heat of human connection.

In the initial phone conversation, we may not bare our soul. However, the more we talk, the more we do. We are always talking about ourselves, even when we're not talking about ourselves. And the same follows for anyone else, the more they talk, the more they share themselves. As we talk on the phone, we're reconnecting with someone we use to have a connection with. And there are some expectations here. First, there is the current expectation of connection. This person is a person we had good conversation with. Our interaction with them was pleasant and light. There were no drama or issues. We were able to discuss various topics and there was no pressure for anything more. We, therefore, expect our interaction to continue along the same lines and if something changes, we expect the change to be mutual. Moreover, we enjoyed our conversation with them. We laughed. We thought and we were intrigued. We made a connection and it was the sort of connection we were looking for. Therefore, we would like that connection to continue. Secondly, we look at our history as another point of connection. We expect them to be able to connect with us because they were able to connect with us once upon a time. They used to know our habits. They used to understand how we did things and why. They used to know what irritated us and what made us the world's happiest person. And though they are an ex-lover now, to some small degree, we still expect them to be able to connect with us on some level because of that history. No matter if we've changed or not, we still have that expectation.

Which leads me to this point: these expectations open us up for transparency and thus - vulnerability. We talk and they talk. We share and they share. The both of us can play games only for so long before the real conversation begins. And the more we have these phone conversations and these late night chats, the more we have to entertain those unwelcomed questions. We have to address those unwelcomed questions because we are getting precisely what we wanted – someone who knows us. And in knowing us, we are getting that intimacy we desire. Someone is paying attention to our mannerisms. Someone is picking up on our voice tone changes. Someone is hearing the different words we use for different moods. Phone calls minimize the distractions of non-verbal chat. We can focus on the conversation easier without paying attention to what people are doing while they're saying something because we can't see them. While there is non-verbal communication happening on the phone call, it is minimized. And while we're talking, they're paying attention to not only our words but also the choice of our words and how we speak our words. We're the source of their attention and WE LOVE IT! We love it because they're connecting with us, which motivates us to talk to them more and connect with them too. And when they raise those unwelcomed inquiries, we hesitate and eventually breakdown and answer them. We tell them about the setback. We tell them how we don't want to deal with it. We tell them how we feel. We speak about why we cry. We explain our insecurities and we connect even the more. They tell us its ok. They encourage us. They speak sweet words of affirmation. They tell us how they see us in their eyes. And we become overwhelmed by their kindness and where slowly breaking down. Our guard is coming down. Our defensiveness is being won over. The heat of their concerned conversation is warming our hearts and stimulating our minds. We like them making us feel good. We like them affirming our personhood. And we're beginning to like them all over again.

And here at this point, we try to pump our brakes. We try to remind ourselves this is a person we used to have history with and the relationship went wrong. We try to stack the deck against them based on the past and not now. We try remembering why we broke up. We try conjuring up those emotions but we can't help but to enjoy the feeling we have right now, the feeling of connection we have. Part of us says, "*This ain't gonna work*" and the other side says, "*Who knows what the future holds*". We are wrestling back and forth with ourselves now. We're trying to reconcile the feelings we're developing in context with our history. It doesn't match but we continue talking to them on the phone. Some have told us to not engage in this, but we ignore them. We ignore them because we're EXPERIENCING REAL HEAT! We're connecting with someone in an intimate way during a time we felt we couldn't connect with anyone else (regardless of the fact we detached from everyone). Rather than to listen to their reasoning, we shut down our allies and friends because it's going against what we're feeling. We like our heat. We need our heat. This is real fire from a past flame and we're not letting anyone take it away from us. Who cares if we didn't work out before, we have heat now! Who cares if we cried and had our heart broken before, we have a real connection now! Yes, we're defensive of our fire! Yes, we're guarding our heat! And yes, if we have to choose between our friends and teammates or the person who's giving us fire and heat, the sad reality is most of us in the heat of the moment, will choose real heat from past flames than current help propelling us into our future success.

Some of us are slowly losing ourselves in our reconnection with old relationships and it is not a surprise. It's not a surprise because we set the situation up for it. We've disconnected from our allies. That action positioned us to connect with something else. The more we disconnected from people we knew, the more our need for intimate connection became apparent. Now we are starving for affirmation and we will accept whatever attention we can get because we have positioned ourselves to be in such a predicament. And we have no clue that we are steadily setting the stage for our situation to become worse than it already is.

Moreover, phone calls are what I call "***stage setters***". Whether people realize it or not, phone calls can be used to put someone in a certain mind frame for the face-to-face visit. I have used phone calls to have people think about the things I want them to think about. This way when they see me, they're thinking about my topics. Phone calls are a way to set the mental environment of a person's thought. When you say something they like, people remember the tone of your voice, how you said it and what you said. They will remember the feeling they felt when they heard it. And if it's a good feeling, they'll rehearse the entire event over and over again as a prelude to your face-to-face visit. Ultimately, they will want in reality the picture you've painted in their mind. The rehearsal of such an event sets the stage for what happens next. And once you've been on the phone for so long, eventually, you will reach the conclusion that a face-to-face visit is not a nice suggestion; IT'S A DEFINITE NECESSITY!

Knowing this, phone calls can become risky business. To create a good mental picture in a person's mind, words are not merely enough. One needs to tailor the words he/she speaks and the picture being painted to the person's appetite he/she is speaking to. When someone knows us, they know how and what they need to say and do to maneuver us to the next step. Some may do it by accident, while others know exactly what they're doing. This is a dangerous place to be because the person on the phone is using the phone to touch our "hot" buttons, particularly the buttons igniting sexual desire. They know how to put us in the mood. They know what we like to hear and how we like to hear it. Moreover, we have history. This is not someone we just met, but someone we've sexed before. Once in this mindset, we are no longer referencing imagination: we're tapping into deeply buried memories. And once these memories are unearthed, our situation has just become all the more complicated and irrational. Our emotions run without restraint. Our passions start driving us. We crave what we haven't had in a long time. We miss the ecstasy. We yearn for the touch of intimacy (sexual intimacy). On the phone, the stage is being set for our face-to-face visits and once there, we'll no longer talk about it. We'll be doing it and thus our situation becomes worse.

STOP!

BREATHE DEEP! & CONSIDER!

1. Has continual phone conversations with your past romance changed your mind over time? If so, how?

2. Have any of your phone conversations started out non-sexual and became sexual? Why did it happen? Did you start out resisting and later on engaged in it? Why?

3. How has talking on the phone with the same person affected your life?

THE VISITS

All the phone conversations have culminated to these moments, back to being face-to-face. Except this time around, our minds have significantly changed from the initial encounter. In the initial encounter, we were shocked and surprised by our past lover being in the same building as we were. We played games as if we didn't know them and we were careful with how we portrayed our connection to them. This time around, we want them and we don't care what others think. We are ready to go out with them, dance with them, and have fun with them, kiss them, hug them, and even make love to them. If there is anything certain, we are certain we want them in our lives because we have real fire from our past flames. We have real energy from a real connection and our identities are redefined and renewed because of their presence in our lives. Without them, we feel we would not be here and we are willing and ready to give them our hearts, our minds, our souls, and our bodies. This is real fire for us and we are ready to sing like Anita Baker "Rapture of Love". Yes, WE ARE TRULY CAUGHT UP!

Let's not get this twisted. Most of us just don't jump off the phone into the bedroom (though there are some of us who have). This has a process too. Usually, we start off testing the waters. We remember the conversations on the phone and the flirting that took place but we're not high school kids wet behind the ears. We know plenty of people who talk a good game and they aren't about anything. You know those types of people who are "***all lip and no action***". We entertain each other. Movies, dinners, plays, comedy shows, concerts, and even church are just some of the avenues we explore with them to see what they are really about. We're trying to match the idea of who they portrayed themselves to be on the phone compared to our time spent with them in person. We want to know if we are fooling ourselves or if this is real. We want to make sure the person of today is not the same person of yesterday, for if they are, then we want nothing to do with them because that's why we didn't work out the first time around. However, we love the feeling we have while we're in their presence. We love how they make us feel. It's as if when we are with them, there is not a care in the world. Life is good with them. And the further time extends, the more we connect with them in ways words cannot express.

Throughout all of this, we're slowly entering a different realm of relationship. We're hugging longer. We're losing ourselves in their eyes more. We touch each other softly igniting a feeling rendering us speechless. Their touch alone is so electrifying. All we want is to be consumed in the other's presence. We kiss more and more. We spend time with each other more and more. And though we try to stay away from the bedroom, we desire within ourselves the kind of intimacy shared in the bedroom. The kind of intimacy shared between husband and wife. The kind of intimacy belonging to couples in love with one another and trusting each other completely. The kind of intimacy shared between two people who are both each other's best friend. We want that intimacy. We want the sort of love making that is birthed from such a connection. We desire the fire of that intimacy. We know we don't want sex. We don't want the meaningless, short lived, physical activity leaving us robbed of our time and our dignity. We want something much more meaningful, fulfilling, and long lasting. We want something caressing our hearts, stimulating our minds, and explosive to our souls. And we feel we have found the fulfillment of that desire in a past lover who is now again our new lover. And we give them ourselves, and we make love.

At this point, I believe I need to draw some distinctions. Lines need to be drawn to clearly understand where I'm going with this whole discussion. I will define the difference in sexual intercourse and lovemaking and I will distinguish the lines between making love to a person versus making love to an idea. On a side note: *Of the many opinions & perspectives on these subject matters, I claim not to speak as if my opinion is law. Different people will have different rationales for the matters I discuss. However, I do assert my position from my experience and the experience of others. And therefore, I share this with those who are open to discover something they may not know or to redefine ideas they may already know.*

- **LOVEMAKING**

  First, many of us understand and believe there is difference between sex and lovemaking. Some us feel we've never made love, but simply had endless experiences of sex, while others of us feel we've had both and prefer the latter. One thing is certain: whether we've had both, had one or the other, or never experienced either, we know at some fundamental level, there is a difference. And the difference is **lovemaking is the ongoing experience encompassing the whole person (spirit, soul, and body) produced out of a person's sincere and intimate connection with another manifesting in a variety of ways including but not limited to sexual activity.** Lovemaking is not just sex, but it is so much more. Lovemaking is total embracing. Lovemaking doesn't pick and choose what it likes and dislikes. Lovemaking embraces everything. It just doesn't focus on our bodies. Lovemaking touches our thoughts, calms our fears, embraces our emotions, silences our anger, uplifts our soul, and strengthens our spirit. Lovemaking is the totality of human connection. It is the climax of human relationships. Therefore, when our bodies explode with sexual climaxes during the sexual activity of lovemaking, it is not just our bodies peaking with satisfaction; it is our total being peaking with satisfaction. Our entire personhood is raptured in the tangible, sexual part of lovemaking because our entire personhood has made a connection and has been satisfied.

  Moreover, lovemaking is an ongoing connection. When we make love, we connect. That's what making love is. It's an intimate connection at it's best. The beauty about lovemaking is it happens in the bedroom and out of the bedroom as well. Honestly, lovemaking should and must spend the majority of its development out of the bedroom anyway. When a couple can only connect with each other in the bedroom, there is a problem and it needs to be addressed. Lovemaking should always be happening. Across the room, we should be able to touch each other. Over the phone, we should be able kiss each other. Writing letters, we should be able to hold each other. Even to the degree we sleep alone, we should still feel our significant other's presence. We should hear their voice when they're sleeping. When we're in a struggle, we should be able to hear the affirmation of our personhood when they actually are completely clueless to our predicament. Lovemaking doesn't end when the orgasms are over because lovemaking has no end (if it's truly lovemaking). That's why we call it "**lovemaking,**" because we're always loving and always connecting.

Lovemaking is SELFLESS. Our concerns are for the other. Our efforts are for the other. We belong to each other not out of obligation. Duty and obligation are not the platform on which lovemaking stands. We belong to each other out of the selfless giving of ourselves to each other. We give because we love. We love and therefore we give. Loving and giving walk hand-in-hand. If man tells a woman he loves her but he's stingy, then the validity of his love will certainly be questioned. Likewise, if a woman continually takes and never gives but claims to love, where is the validation of her love? The tangible manifestation of lovemaking is selfless giving.

The conversation on lovemaking cannot be complete without defining love. As a child and even as an adult, I've heard so many times from preachers "*God is love*". And while that is the simplest and most complete definition of love (in my opinion), allow me to unpackage the definition of love a little more in depth. <u>**Love is the intimate connection to a person's totality, the acceptance thereof, and the passionate commitment thereto**</u>. Real love embraces real people. Love embraces all that we are and all that we aren't. There is no discrimination in the matter. Love embraces all of us, accepts all of us, and commits to all of us. While there may be things we do to get on each other's nerves, love dislikes the action but embraces the person. Love has the ability to separate the action from the person. My mother has told me many of times as a kid,

"Phillip, I love you but I don't like you". What she was really saying was her love embraced me totally but she didn't like or condone my behavior. She didn't stop loving me because I was being disobedient. She disapproved my behavior. My mother's love for me embraced my ability to do right and wrong. She knew what I was capable of and loved me just the same. Love is truly all encompassing.

Love is not ignorant. It knows who we are and accepts us just as we are. Oftentimes, people ask me do I believe in love at first sight and I reply, *"No"*. When they seem surprised by my response and ask why, I reply, *"Because for me to love someone means to know them* (by connection), *accept who they are, and commit to them. A person cannot possibly do all of that at first sight, therefore, it cannot be love"*. Furthermore, I do believe a person can see someone at first sight and realize there is some sort of connection between him or her. That's not a crazy notion at all. It actually happens quite often among all of us. However, while the reality of connecting with someone may be apparent, determining the depth of that connection and discovering who that person truly is has yet to become clear. Therefore, it's wisdom to acknowledge the connection (if but to ourselves only) and exercise patience in discovering what it is we really feel. Again, love is not ignorant and while we may have this wonderful feeling about this person we've seen for the first time, there is much we still don't know about them. So it behooves us to be patient in our pursuit lest we put the cart before the horse and ruin a potentially wonderful relationship before it ever has a chance of becoming a relationship.

Love is not blind. Our weaknesses are just as much part of us as our strengths. When someone loves us, they truly see both. That's the secret of intimacy and love. To be truly intimate means to truly be naked. Only when we can show whom we truly (both the bad and the good) can we really know if someone loves us. When we drop the ball and someone still say "I love you nonetheless", is the assurance we have the one we love truly loves us. They can deal with our imperfections. They can accept our issues. They can be alright with us as we wrestle with our insecurities. They see us for our good and our bad, our success and our shortcomings and the beauty of such intimacy is they still say to us, "*I still choose you*". Can there even be a sweeter notion? What gesture is greater than that? My friend, I submit to you, there is no greater compliment than to be accepted for who we truly are and chosen to be loved by someone above all others. There is no gesture greater than such. And out of such love and intimacy is why lovemaking is the ongoing experience encompassing the whole person (spirit, soul, and body) produced out of a person's sincere and intimate connection with another manifesting in a variety of ways including but not limited to sexual activity.

STOP!

BREATHE DEEP! & CONSIDER!

1. What is your personal definition for lovemaking? Why is that your definition?

2. How do you personally define love? From what experiences do you build that definition?

3. Are you afraid to be transparent and vulnerable in your romantic relationships? Why?

4. In your current/previous relationships (where they said they loved you), did you feel they loved all of you or just part of you? Explain.

5. Do you love people for all they are and all they aren't? How so?

- **SEX**

Contrary to the definition of lovemaking, <u>**sex is simply the participating of a short-lived, physical activity for the purpose of attaining one's own physical gratification**</u>. Sex is simple. It's physical activity. No emotions are needed. No thoughts are required. No one cares about the totality of the individual's personhood. No one is interested in being transparent and having an intimate connection is not necessary. Sex is sex. There is no magic to it. When we're hungry, we eat food. When we're sleepy, we go to bed. And when we're sexually aroused, we have sex. And like everything else, after we've had a good sleep, we move on. After we've had sex, we move on too. For some of us, sex was nothing more than just an activity we used to get what we wanted.

Some of us have labeled sex fun. We've labeled it fun because it came with no responsibility for the other person. We could be reckless and carefree and not have to deal with the burden of emotional attachment. We could get in and get out. We were able to do what we wanted to do, how we wanted to do it, when we wanted to do it, and with whom we wanted to do it, and after we were finished we could move on. Consequently, sex does the exact reverse of lovemaking, minimizing a person to nothing more than a means to an end. For men having sex, women exist for their pleasure. For women having sex, men exist for the same. Sex reduces people from being people to becoming nothing more than a tool. We become as special to people, as a spoon is good for eating cereal. And if we're lucky, some of us even graduated to becoming a favorite spoon for people. Having sex with someone makes the person entitled to feel nothing for the person because he/she didn't need to have feelings to have sex in the first place. All they needed was space and opportunity. In many cases, people having sex don't even need to be sexually aroused. Some people have sex merely because it's available. Sex does not accept the responsibility of caring for another because sex is, has been and always will be – A SELFISH ACT.

Yes my friend, sex is selfish. Sex is all about "**getting mines**". For a prostitute, sex is used to make "her money". For a pimp, sex is the opportunity to make "his money". For strippers, they sell the idea of sex to make "their money". Sex is selfishness. That's why people have one- night stands. That's why guys kick women out of their houses at 2am in the morning after women have sexually satisfied them. Sex has no remorse and it is quite selfish. For women reading this book, how many times did you (or someone you know) get frustrated, aggravated, and even angry because the man you were having sex with climaxed before you did and he was done while you laid there completely unsatisfied? For the men, how many times have you (or someone you know) become disappointed with a woman you were having sex with because the pleasure wasn't as fulfilling as you expected it to be? If sex requires no feelings, then why do the women "feel" anger and why do the men "feel" disappointment? The reasons any of us would feel anything in sex is because WE DIDN'T GET WHAT WE WANTED!

Now here's when the waters get muddy and confusing. Sex is simple and most people act as simple as sex is. However, there those who have graduated from the simplicity of sexual behavior to more complicated behaviors confusing us as to rather we just had sex or were we made love to. In most cases, when men want sex, it's pretty obvious. We tend to play with women focusing on the "**sexual targets**" such as the hips, the breasts, the butt, etc. We also tend to stare. We look at women's lips and focus on their cleavage. However, when we (men) graduate from such elementary behavior, it becomes more difficult to tell what our motives truly are. We still stare but we don't drool over women's cleavage anymore. We gaze into their eyes. We don't reach for women's butts. We place our hands on their lower back gently. Our conversation transitions from sexual to romantic. We engage women in conversations, particular taking interests in their ideas and opinions.

For there are some men who know that women want someone to be interested in them for whom they are. Some of these men know women want to be treated with as much respect after sex as they had before. As a matter of fact, some men know women internally wrestle with the question, *"Will he respect me after I have sex with him"*. And after they have sex with the man, he gives her the respect she was afraid of losing. There are some men who know women want their minds stimulated and the hearts intrigued before their bodies are touched. These same women believe that's how love is supposed to be (and the women who believe such notions are absolutely correct). However, what these types of men do is they duplicate the action without the intent. They stimulate the mind, intrigue the heart and never touch the body but they've no interest in loving the woman. It's still just for sex. These men know women want to be kissed during intercourse so they kiss you. They know you want your back kissed, so they kiss it. They know you want your body explored, so they explore it. They know what you like, so they give it to you. They know you want them to take their time, speed up, slow down, pull your hair, smack your rear end, talk dirty, talk sweet, moan loudly, whisper softly and the list goes on and on. And so it follows, they give you all that you want and the end result is you're sexually satisfied, but you're completely clueless as to what's really happening.

The truth of the matter is it's still just sex. The sex may have been good sex, but its just sex. You may have never been touched that way or taken in that type of manner but when the deed is done, it's still just a short lived physical activity for the purpose of one's own physical gratification. It's still just sex. So how is it so many women are confused about if it was sex or lovemaking? Well, the answer is complicated but I'll make it simple. YOU WERE SOLD A LIE! And here's how you bought the lie. First, he gave you everything that you wanted. How did he know? Simple, you told him. You told him your desires and your dreams. You told him your struggles and pain. You opened your emotions to him and he gave you back the action you desired without the motive you assumed to automatically come with it. He listened without caring. He held you without holding your interests. As a result, you grew connected to what he was portraying to you while never knowing who he was. You connected to his image and not his person.

Secondly, you were his client. He got you to do what he wanted you to do because you misread his affection for you as if it was personal. It wasn't. His affection and attention in you was because you were his CUSTOMER. And as it is in the business world, if you want to keep the ongoing business of your customer, then always remember, "THE CUSTOMER IS ALWAYS RIGHT". He made you feel like you could do no wrong, even when it was your fault. When you had a grievance, he took care of it. When you had an issue, he addressed it. And in return, he kept your business. Your legs stayed open to him. You kept giving him what he wanted because you believed he was giving you what you wanted.

Thirdly, his selfishness was camouflaged in his affection. He wasn't going to be a minuteman. He knew that's not what you wanted. He knew you wanted him to take his time. As you gave him direction, he was careful to give you what you wanted. Why would he do that if he were selfish about his? He did this because he knew the greater your satisfaction was, the greater you would sex him to make his satisfaction awesome. He knew being selfish would minimize his satisfaction. Therefore, he chose to maximize his effort and concentrate his energy on you. His attitude is "why try to satisfy myself when I really want her to do it for me". So he gave you selflessly in order to selfishly experience more. The more he pleased you, the more you pleased him. These men camouflaged their selfishness in their affection, thus misleading women by their affection and making women believe a lie.

STOP!

BREATHE DEEP! & CONSIDER!

1. Have you ever been confused as to whether you just had sex or made love? Why?

2. Have people ever manipulated your romantic desires for their advantage? What happened?

3. Despite your horrible romantic experiences, do you have the courage to believe there are good people who will not hurt you in ways you've already been hurt? Why?

So many of us have been in those situations. And it's not exclusive to women only, but men have experienced the same. We have had women cuddle up with us touch, act friendly, and make us feel like the king of the universe. And after it was over, our hearts connected with someone who was only interested in our body. It goes to show that no one is safe from such disappointment and such people. All of us have been hurt and all of us must continue pressing forward.

- **MAKING LOVE TO IDEAS**

    So now that we've drawn the lines between sex and lovemaking, we must draw the lines between making love to a person versus making love to an idea. Lovemaking to a person has already been addressed a couple of pages ago. We are open to them and they are open to us. We have the truth about each other and it's ok. We accept each other for who each other is and we commit to each other daily. We're naked and not ashamed. We connect with each other in person and when separate. We're physical, emotional, mental, social, environmental, spiritual and sexual. We are totally ourselves and we embrace each other totally. We are not making love to an idea but a real person who is the best person in the world for us and the same person who can function our last nerve. We see a complete picture of them and they of us – and we both choose each other.

However, lovemaking to an idea is altogether a different matter. Here we don't see the other person for who they are. At this point, we see the other person for what they could be. Rather than accepting the person for what they are no matter how ugly or pretty, we choose to look at them for what we think they can become. Herein lies the danger of lovemaking to an idea. We are treating a person not on his/her own merit but the merit of what he/she can potentially become. Lovemaking to an idea denies the person we say we love of who they truly are. Indirectly, we are declaring, "*who you are currently is not good enough, but who I think you can become is worthy of my affection*". So the first thing we need to know about lovemaking to the idea of a person is that it's NOT lovemaking at all – it's still just sex!

While men are known for playing the game of sex, women are known for playing the game of lovemaking to the idea of a real man. Just like sex, lovemaking to the idea of a man minimizes the man for who he is. He is not the future. He is now. If you can't celebrate him now, what makes you believe you can celebrate him when he arrives at whatever place you think he should be? In the sex section, I emphatically declare you were bamboozled and hoodwinked. However, in this section, with the same emphasis declare, you have deceived yourself and denied yourself potential happiness merely because you can't accept a man for who he is and where he is.

Lovemaking to an idea is leap frogging a person into a future that may not be a future at all. There may be some who attempt to twist my concept of our dreams and manipulate it for this section. So allow me to clear the matter. I believe when it comes to our dreams; we need to use them for direction and a standard. Dreams are the direction we choose to pursue that guides our lives. Dreams also are the standard by which we need to live our lives now, so we can reach our dreams later. However, lovemaking the idea of a person is not the same. None of us can force a person to do anything regardless of what we may see about them. The dreams applicable to us work because those are realities within our control. We can control our actions. We can choose our choices. We can control the decisions impacting our lives. However, when it comes to another person, we can't control what they do no matter how much of an influence we are in their lives. We are still just an INFLUENCE. Therefore, lovemaking the idea of the person is directly believing we have the power to make them something they may never be. And such an assumption means we've failed to have faith and we believe we have the power to change things we truly have no power to change. We have deceived ourselves. We have minimized others in the name of loving their potential and disrespecting their present. MY FRIEND, THIS IS NOT LOVE. IT IS SELFISHNESS CAMOUFLAGED!

STOP!

BREATHE DEEP! & *CONSIDER!*

1. Have you been guilty of loving the idea of a person rather than loving the person? Why?

2. What about the person's present made you not want to acknowledge it?

3. What about the person's future made you want to treat him/her according to it?

4. Why did you choose to stay when it would have been easier to find someone you could be happy with their present?

Dealing with the visits from past flames are real issues. Some people are playing games with us. Some are good and others are novices. Some we can see coming afar off and others we don't know what the damage is until they're long gone. Some people have deceived us intentionally in order to satisfy their own selfish urges. Others have deceived themselves and minimized us because they were selfish. They didn't want to see their deception because they felt entitled. While on the phone, we talked about sex, but when we started having those visits, sex became love. We're not sure where we went wrong. Some of us aren't sure how we could love someone who didn't love us. We're not sure how it happened. We've detached from our friends and our allies. We ignored our team and dismissed their advice. We wanted romance and intimacy. We wanted fire and passion. And everything we asked for, we received only to realize now that it's ours, we don't want it. And now, we're more confused than when we started. There's a reality hitting us square in face and we're not quite sure what it is. We feel a tugging in our souls but we don't know what it is. We're discouraged more now than when we started. Once again, we feel cold and this time we're not looking for intimacy. Something is making us restless. We can't reconcile what happened and yet something inside of us won't be still either. What is this feeling I have? What is this urge within me? What is this tugging in my soul?

THE REALITY

My friend, the reality is your dreams are still calling out to you. The abundant life you started pursuing in Chapter 1 is still beckoning you to pick yourself up and press forward. Yes, you were side tracked by your desire for intimacy. Hence, why I took this chapter as a side note to Chapter 6 dealing with setbacks. You are not alone in such a matter. I have been where you are. I have also made similar mistakes. Nonetheless, my life was still calling me to BREATHE DEEP. Otherwise, to remain in this place would mean I would die shallow. Just as my future called out to me, your future is calling out to you. LISTEN TO IT! Don't make excuses about what happened. LISTEN TO YOUR FUTURE!

Let's get down to business now. The point of this section is to RESET us. We've allowed our setbacks to throw us off course and here's how. We were upset about whatever went wrong. We never faced it but we chose to run from it instead. We disconnected from our friends who encourage us. We detached from our allies who invested in us. And we've separated from the team supporting us (the same team we spent so much time developing). We chose to isolate ourselves and we blamed the setback for our decisions. The setback did not make our choices – WE DID. We are the blame for stuff going wrong. While we may not have had control of the setback going wrong, we are responsible for allowing the setback to remain a setback. We lost our perspective. And since we isolated ourselves from friends, we started looking for other support. Conveniently as it may have been, the reason past lovers have such a significant impact (generating real heat) is because we have abandoned the heat of our friends and stopped making heat ourselves. We stopped taking the initiative in our lives. We stopped surrounding ourselves with people who held us accountable for what we said we would do.

I know, you didn't want to be reminded of the setback, but here's the reality – YOU NEEDED TO BE REMINDED! You needed to be reminded so you could deal with it and move on. They needed to remind you that you weren't the only one experiencing the setback. People have invested in us AND WE FORGOT THAT! People have put the dollars behind our names AND WE FORGOT THAT! People have spent their time, their energies, and their resources to help us achieve AND WE FORGOT THAT! We acted as if our pain was the only pain! We minimized the sacrifice of others for us. We blatantly disregarded the efforts of those who've proven their trustworthiness by cutting them out of our lives! WE BECAME SELFISH! AND WE'RE REVERTING BACK TO THE SHALLOW PERSPECTIVES AND MEANINGLESS BEHAVIORS WE DESPERATELY WANTED TO ESCAPE FROM!

We owe some people major apologies. We've inflicted damage on some of our most trusted friends for no other reason than simply being selfish. Yes, it's an ugly reality, but a reality nonetheless. To ignore this fact would be more devastating than the first mistake. We cannot take advantage of our friends, disregard our allies, blow off their support and believe saying "I'm sorry" will make things better. THIS IS REAL LIFE! We've got to meet them face-to-face and admit the wrong decisions we made. We've lost some respect from some people and we have to go back and correct our errors. It's not easy, but it's necessary. People respect others who can admit when they're wrong. It may sound like a cliché and if it is, then it's an accurate cliché. If we can be honest with ourselves, then we can be honest with others. And when people can see that we can be honest with them, they will have the confidence to be honest with us. And here's a quick FYI (for your information), we may not like what they have to say when they're honest, but we need to be able to hear what they have to say. Again, remember, they're not our enemies; they're our allies. Sometimes the truth hurts but it's the good kind of pain. It's the kind of pain reminding us not to make this mistake again. **If we cannot allow our friends, allies, and supporters to hold us accountable, who can hold us accountable?**

I spend so much time talking about reconciling our relationships with our teams because they've helped us get this far and in this chapter we simply acted stupid. And in acting stupid I mean we became emotionally consumed because a problem happened and we got reckless. When we separated from our allies, we separated from real intimacy. Do you think your people really love EVERYTHING you do? Did you honestly believe they endorsed EVERY IDEA, EVERY ACTION, and EVERY DECISION you made? As rhetorical as these questions may be, allow me to answer the obvious nonetheless. NO!!!

THEY DON'T LIKE EVERYTHING YOU DO! My people don't like every decision I make. They don't agree with every action I take. And a lot of the ideas I had, they shot them down! Because people support you doesn't mean they romanticize you! Hence, this why I say when we abandon our team, we abandon real intimacy. I say this because they see we don't know everything. They see we don't have all the answers. They know we make bad decisions. They know all about our filthy mouths, our attitudes, our personal issues and our individual idiosyncrasies; and they still choose to support us. They still choose to rally behind our dreams. They still choose to spend money on our behalf because they believe in us. They know our current issues. They believe in our future and they ACCEPT US FOR WHO WE TRULY ARE! That's the beauty of such relationships. And that is exactly what REAL INTIMACY IS! IT "GET'S" NO BETTER THAN THAT!

So go back to your team, my friend, and make amends. Fix your mistakes and clean up your mess. These people have respected you. It's about time you give them their respect. Show them why they believed in you. Remind them of the caliber of man or woman you truly are. Show them you can admit that you're wrong. And show them that it's not beyond you to ask for help. Show them you truly are sorry for hurting them. Show them you are considerate of them. Show them you're not running away from the problem but facing it head on. Show them you're not a coward but a man of integrity and a woman of dignity. Show them you are BREATHING DEEP and you refuse to die shallow! My friend, show them what you're truly made of!

Now concerning your past flame, I must ask you some questions.

STOP!

BREATHE DEEP! & CONSIDER!

1. Would you have been in a different mindset to deal with your past flame had you not ran from your problems and abandoned your team? Why?

2. Would your need for romantic intimacy differ had you not separated yourself from the intimacy of your friends and allies? Why?

3. Will your past flame be able to deal with the new you restored, which is significantly different to the old you wounded (the you they met)? Why?

Loving someone is never an easy subject to discuss. All of us have different experiences with love. Telling someone how to love is the equivalent of telling someone how to taste food. All of us have different tastes; therefore, all of us will taste differently. Nonetheless, it's subject matter we must discuss. I will deal with this as delicately as I can while simultaneously being as clear as possible. With past flames, there comes a reality we must take note of. The reality is their romance and influence in our lives is PAST. They are our history. They're our yesterday. And so when a past flame is kindling real and current heat, the question arises – why? How can we kindle wood already burnt start a fire again? The reality is it can't unless someone places a fire under it again. Now personally, I'm not an advocate of jumpstarting old romantic relationships. However, I also do believe some relationships don't work because the timing was off. In those cases, some may come back together in a different point in time and workout completely fine because the timing was better. However, in most cases, that's not the case. Therefore, when relationships go wrong and people come back together, we must ask ourselves, *"What is it that I want that makes me believe they can give it to me now whereby in times past, they couldn't?"* If they were able to give us something, then why the break up in the first place? Do we just want to rationalize sex as making love to the idea of what we want? If so, it's still just sex with a lie.

Dealing with our past flames begins with facing with us first. All of us want romantic intimacy. That's normal. We all want to be kissed, held, touched and experience lovemaking too. However, before we can accept the intimacy of others, we must be intimate with ourselves. We must accept us for all that we are and all that we aren't. We must love ourselves. Breathing Deep first starts with us. We have friends and allies helping us and that's great. But we can never forget that this journey is and always will be OUR JOURNEY. Our friends can't fight our battles – we fight them. We make the decisions for our lives and we write our own destinies. No one else has that right. And when our lives are over, we are responsible for what we did with it. Our romantic relationships (like every other relationship) should add to us, not control us. Romantic relationships should add depth to who we are. They should not control our lives. It doesn't mean we won't make decisions in favor of preserving our romantic interests, for we will. However, it does mean we make decisions for our loved ones because we love them and our relationships are important, but not because they control us.

This is your life, my friend. This life is a new life. Yesterday's tactics won't work today. Last year's warmth won't address this year's winter. **The reality is past flames can't warm you in the way you need because you are in a new place**. You're a new man. You're a new woman. If they couldn't keep up with you before you started this journey, what makes you think they can keep up now? You need fresh heat. You need to go back and start your own fire. Remember how to encourage yourself. Do not hand over your tools to someone who doesn't have the expertise in encouraging you like yourself. Remember, every now and again, you have to be your own cheerleader. If you lose your voice, how can you hear your own encouragement? Encourage yourself! Strengthen yourself. Affirm yourself and warm yourself. Set yourself on fire once again.

STOP!

BREATHE DEEP! & CONSIDER!

1. Is your past flame adding depth to your new life? How?

2. Is your past flame pursuing a goal compatible with yours? What is it? How is it compatible?

3. What kind of heat is your past flame generating? Is that the kind of heat you need to get you to reach your dreams successfully? Why? _____

We've started this process by first looking at ourselves. We must not stop now. We can't hand over the keys of our life to someone just because they're giving us romance and intimacy or just sex. Sex is not good enough to forfeit what we took so long preparing for. We can't allow past flames to stifle our success. We can't hide behind relationships while the real issues affecting our lives go unaddressed. In doing so, we hurt our chances of overcoming even more because we disregard and offend those who truly can help us and we trade them in for a mirage of what we think we want. Only when we get close enough do we discover what we thought we had was still - just a mirage. Let's learn from our mistakes and press forward to the end. We have come this far, why stop now? Don't you agree? THIS IS OUR REALITY. And who knows, the romance you desire may be closer to you than you think.

Chapter 7
Intimacy Reality Check

We've spent a considerable amount of time looking at how romantic relationships can throw us off. Let's work through these questions and see if we can avoid some of the pitfalls I've mentioned earlier. Our lives are too precious to hide in pretentious relationships. We need real heat, real intimacy, and real companionship. This may be a little difficult but as I said before, you've made it this far, why stop now? This is our reality check. Let's take our time. Take a deep breath my friend and face the questions of your romance.

1. Have you isolated yourself because of how your setback made you feel? Why?

2. Have you blamed your setback for where you currently are in your life? Why?

3. Have you been looking for romance to substitute your team and validate your escape? Why?

4. How did you initially feel when you reconnected with a past romance? Why?

5. What was your context during the time you met your past romance? How did that affect your interaction with him/her?

6. Was the conversation refreshing? Why or why not?

7. Did you exchange contact information with them? Why?

8. What do you expect to happen between you and your past romance? Why?

9. Has continual phone conversations with your past romance changed your mind over time? If so, how?

10. Have any of your phone conversations started out non-sexual and became sexual? Why did it happen? Did you start out resisting and later on engaged in it? Why?

11. How has talking on the phone with the same person affected your life?

12. What is your personal definition for lovemaking? Why is

that your definition?

13. How do you personally define love? From what experiences do you build that definition?

14. Are you afraid to be transparent and vulnerable in your romantic relationships? Why?

15. In your current/previous relationships (where they said they loved you), did you feel they loved all of you or just part of you? Explain.

16. Do you love people for all they are and all they aren't? How so?

17. Have you ever been confused as to whether you just had sex or made love? Why?

18. Have people ever manipulated your romantic desires for their advantage? What happened?

19. Despite your horrible romantic experiences, do you have the courage to believe there are good people who will not hurt you in ways you've already been hurt? Why?

20. Have you been guilty of loving the idea of a person rather than loving the person? Why?

21. What about the person's present made you not want to acknowledge it?

22. What about the person's future made you want to treat him/her according to it?

23. Why did you choose to stay when it would have been easier to find someone you could be happy with their present?

24. Would you have been in a different mindset to deal with your past flame had you not ran from your problems and abandoned your team? Why?

25. Would your need for romantic intimacy differ had you not separated yourself from the intimacy of your friends and allies? Why?

26. Will your past flame be able to deal with the new you restored, which is significantly different to the old you wounded (the you they met)? Why?

27. Is your past flame adding depth to your new life? How?

28. Is your past flame pursuing a goal compatible with yours? What is it? How is it compatible?

29. What kind of heat is your past flame generating? Is that the kind of heat you need to get you to reach your dreams successfully? Why?

CHAPTER 8

THIS IS MY STORY (Chronicling Your Journey)

*"And the LORD answered me, and said, **Write** the vision, and make it plain upon tables, that he may run that readeth it. For the vision is yet for an appointed time, but at the end it shall speak, and not lie: though it tarry, wait for it; because it will surely come, it will not tarry"* (Habakkuk 2:2-3 King James Version).

After athletes have spent so much time training and practicing, they develop behaviors for optimal breathing. Through rigorous exercise, their lungs are conditioned to maximize every opportunity. Consequently, there comes a point in time where athletes no longer practice breathing. They simply just BREATHE!

MY BLOOD, MY SWEAT, MY TEARS

We started this journey remembering where we came from. We looked at our lives and faced our past for what it was. We didn't try to sugarcoat anything. We didn't offer any excuses. We cried. We got angry. We argued within ourselves and we asked why. Yet when we were through everything we could possibly go through, we accepted our past for what it was. Through the process of BREATHING DEEP we came to realize one truth – WE'RE RESPONSIBLE FOR OUR LIVES! We make the choice to breathe deep. We choose if we will die shallow. We chart the course of our lives. We make the decisions impacting others and ourselves. We write our own destinies. This life is our life and this story is our story.

Throughout this book you've written answers to the questions in this book, which directly impact your life. There is another reason for the questions. It wasn't just to make you STOP, BREATHE DEEP & CONSIDER. That was just to tell you how to approach the questions. The questions were designed to give you one more tool in your inventory. I didn't want to just tell you what to do but I wanted to empower you to actually put this tool in use throughout the book. The tool I make reference of is the tool of Vision Planning and Execution. I could have told you what to do in order to transition your dreams into vision planning and execution, but I preferred you started doing it so you could see for yourself that vision planning works. Dreams are the places where we want to go, but vision is the plan and execution actually taking us there. If you have answered these questions as they pertained to you, you should have a clearer understanding of whom you are and where you want to go. You should know some pitfalls as well as the type of people you need to help you. If you've answered these questions, you will know what steps you need to take for your dreams and you should know the areas you need help in. This book is not to coach you to just have dreams; it is written to empower you to write your life's vision with well thought out questions focusing our attention to effectively execute our plan. By doing so, our dreams no longer remain dreams. THEY BECOME OUR LIFE!

And that's what I mean by BREATHE DEEP OR DIE SHALLOW. Life cannot be about dreams only, but action also. We must take action with our dreams. The first action is to WRITE OUR DREAMS DOWN. We must sit down and write our vision. There are no shortcuts. We must sit down and write. As you read these pages, you should have been writing as well. It is in writing whereby we authorize ourselves to pursue our desires. It's in writing where we believe our dreams are real and can become our tangible reality. Writing is our declaration of affirmation. We believe because we write. By our own hand, we accept the reality of our dreams and we take on the responsibility to bring our dreams to fruition. To BREATHE DEEP, WE MUST WRITE!

And when we write, we'll discover something about ourselves. We'll discover what it takes to make our life matter. We'll see what we need to do to make our lives count for more than a catalogue of memories. We'll unearth hidden potential. We'll foresee future problems and we'll develop alternative solutions. When we write, we empower our own hands to take direct care of our lives. In doing something as small as writing, we tip the scales of life in our favor. What we write becomes the measuring stick for our success. We rate ourselves against our words. In writing, we remember what we committed to. We remember our promises. We remember why we started the journey when times get hard and we recall why we won't go back. Writing keeps us accountable (if but to ourselves). Our success is dependant upon us writing. Failure to write our vision is failure to our dreams, our friends, our families, our support, our God, and us. My friend, there is no other way to say this: WE MUST WRITE!

So I say to you, don't just write the vision for your life but WRITE YOUR STORY. Let people read what you came through. Let them read about your blood, sweat and tears. Let them see your life wasn't as easy as they think it was. Write, so they can glean from the lessons of your mistakes and your success. Write, so they can connect with your emotions. Your words will help your readers maneuver through the difficulty of emotions incapable to verbally articulate. If you just write a journal or a diary, you can see your own growth. You can see how you grew from the beginning of this book to the end. You can see where you were a year ago from today. It's such a beautiful thing to capture our lives on the pages. As fast as life comes, we deserve it to snatch as much as we can to savor our experiences. Our life doesn't belong to the pages of time. Our life belongs to those who read the pages of time! I made up my mind that my life will not be just a good story told off of the lips. I want my own children to read my life as my hand writes my life. My legacy is to place my life into the hands of my children so they can know what I did and go further. What do you have to lose? What do you have to fear? People need your story. They need your experiences. Don't be selfish! Share your life. After all, life is not life if it doesn't connect to anyone else. SO WRITE! WRITE THAT POETRY! WRITE THAT SONG! WRITE THAT PLAY! WRITE THAT SPEECH! AND WRITE THAT BOOK!

My friend, chronicling your story is one of the greatest

contributions you could make to your life. It's better than a paycheck and more valuable than any artwork. Your life is timeless and priceless. And once you believe that, those around you will feel their lives are likewise because you make them feel so. Writing changes your perspective. It changes how you respond to things. Writing changes how we feel about things and our ability to see from different vantage points increases significantly. And once you start writing, you can't stop. It's like reading a good book and your life is that book. You're reading an exciting story because it's your story and you're not only reading it but writing it also. THAT'S TRULY EXCITING! You are your own author. So value your own words. Value your opinions. Esteem your ideas. They are good ideas. You have great opinions. There is a secret to writing and only those who dare to write dare to discover.

This life is your life. This is your story. This is your blood, your sweat, and your tears. I have merely served you as your life coach and a friend to help you blossom into the man or woman you desire for yourself. I pray these words have helped you move closer to the fulfillment of your dreams. I believe in you. Now go forth and watch your life transform before your eyes. It's an exciting experience when your life unfolds before your very eyes because it's happening to me as I write to you. And believe me when I say there's nothing like finishing what you started. It's a feeling you can never forget and it's an experience so worth having. My friend, you started this journey and though this life may get hard at times – FINISH WHAT YOU STARTED! Finish it! You're now ready to take the helm from here. I've done my part. I've given you what I could. I think you're ready to tip the scale of life in your favor. And now, with the stage set and your platform built, there's only one thing I can tell you at this point.

BREATHE DEEP!!!

OR

Die Shallow

BREATHE DEEP REPRISE

Chapter 1
Breaking Ground Exercise

Now it is time for you to write. I have brought all the questions I have asked you throughout this chapter back to this page. During the chapter I have asked you to stop, breathe deep, and consider. Here I ask you to stop, breathe deep, and write. Breaking ground is YOUR labor to move you to the place where you want to be. It is interactive. Engage these questions. Think about them. Answer them. If you will write, you will move yourself closer to your dreams. No short cuts to success. My friend, this is work, a work that is worth the effort and time. Invest in yourself. You deserve it. I will see you in the next chapter. NOW BREATHE DEEP & BREAK GROUND!

1. What are 2 experiences you have had and what has been your response to those experiences that now contribute to the way you see life?

2. How has your perspective of life affected your relationships and the way you communicate with other people?

3. Does your perspective make you more trusting of people or more suspicious? Why?

4. Can you see yourself developing a new response to your history? If so, how? If not, why?

5. What are 3 experiences in your life you have a difficult time accepting happened to you?

6. For each experience, what crime was committed against

your heart, your body, your faith, your trust etc causing so much pain to make you want to deny it ever happened?

7. Was your response to each event then out of anger or out of sadness?

8. Is your perspective now bitter, hateful, skeptical, and cynical?

9. Can you see someone being enhanced by your experience if you can find the strength to share it with a hopeful insight?

10. Remember 2 of your dreams; what were they?

11. Are your dreams fulfilled, in development, or shattered? What happened?

12. What are your dreams like now, or do you dream at all?

13. Can you find the courage to dream again?

14. What are 2 abilities I do well?

15. What are 2 inabilities I do not do well?

16. What will turn my weaknesses into strengths?

17. How will my strengths & weaknesses affect my pursuit of my dreams?

18. Regarding my dreams, how can I maximize my strengths and position my weaknesses to become strong?

Breathe Deep Reprise

Chapter 2
Lines in the Sand

We have talked about various ways to identify help. And like chapter 1, I have collected all of the questions in this chapter so you can answer them and begin drawing lines in the sand. Take your time. You are taking a personal position in your life and this position will revolutionize everything you do from here forward. This race is not given to the fastest reader or the strongest writer. This race is given to the one who crosses the finish line with the necessary tools to help you live your life with a little more meaning and significance. SO TAKE A DEEP BREATH, AUTHORIZE YOURSELF & WRITE.

1. Have you taken your dreams public? If so, how? If not, why?

2. Identify 3 people who are supportive of your dreams. In what way does each of them support you?

3. Identify 3 people who are skeptics, cynics, or critics. Has their opinions helped you? If so, how?

4. Identify 3 ways the supportive people differ from your skeptics, cynics, and critics in attitude and behavior.

5. Which groups do you like more spending more of your time around? Why?

6. Identify 3 people who attack you. What is the reason(s) each of them attack you?

7. How have you responded to the attacks in the past? Why?

8. Identify 2 serious attacks. What are they about?

9. Identify 3 people you told your dreams to. What commitments did each of them make to you?

10. Thinking of the same 3 people, how have they fulfilled their commitments to you?

11. Are you satisfied with their effort to perform what each of them promised to you? Why or why not?

12. Who are the "double agents" in your life?

13. Who would you like on your "dream team"? What areas of expertise do you think they will contribute to?

Chapter 3
Personal Face Off

Take your time in answering these questions. It is difficult to come to grip with some of these answers and it will equally be difficult to discover the answers as well. Facing off with ourselves is not easy to do. Often times, we won't like what we see. People are always telling us who we are, what we do wrong, what we said wrong, how we hurt their feelings and more. And in some cases, their assessment about us is correct. Other times its wrong but it's up to us to discover for ourselves. Only when we truly know, can we truly change. If you are like me, it hurts you to know that you hurt your loved one. So let's look ourselves, question-by-question, let's record our answers and face off with ourselves to discover how to cope with frustrating conversations beginning with discovering who we are in relationships. Now my friend, let's write.

1. Have I asked people about who they truly are without asking myself were I ready to be responsible for what I heard?

2. What was my response?

3. What was their response?

4. Have many of my conflicts with others happened because of me misdiagnosing who I thought the person was compared to who they truly were?

5. Do I believe there is a value in discovering who people truly are? Why or why not?

6. Do I practice that conviction? How?

7. What are you "feeling" right now?

8. What are you thinking of right now?

9. What past or recent experiences make me crave being close to someone?

10. Do I spend more time fighting in my relationship than agreeing?

11. Which of the navigational concepts do I most relate to? Why?

12. Do I hold a quiet grudge against my significant other or spouse? What is it? Why?

13. Do I silently despise or dislike my significant other or spouse? How did it happen?

14. Do I have a "Hero's Complex"? Why?

15. Why is it difficult for me to break away from relationships that hurt me?

16. What is it I really want when I have sex? Why?

17. What is it about being alone I'm truly fearful of? Why?

Chapter 4
Achieving Balance

I started this chapter off quoting a Bible verse discussing true balances versus false balances. I shared with you Yoga information regarding when balance is achieved, peace is achieved and when balance is not achieved, conflict occurs. Looking throughout church history, conflict has been apparent. From Christian crusades to tele-evangelical financial scams, we have seen the results of conflict from being without balance. Yet there are also countless other examples where we see peace achieved when churches achieved balance. They invested in life around them rather than operating as a vacuum. Our perspective will determine our action. If we aim to value church for its contribution without minimizing the contributions of others around us, we can achieve balance and peace individually and collectively. But if we continue to believe *"all we need is Jesus and we don't need nobody else"*, then we are sentencing not only ourselves, but also generations to follow a life of conflict and pain with the hope they find their own way without our help. Therefore, take this time to write the answers to the questions we posed before. Take your time and let's achieve balance together. Now STOP, BREATHE DEEP, and WRITE.

1. Do you find yourself becoming bored or easily annoyed with your church? How can you tell?

2. Do you find yourself in conflicts or confrontations at church or about church often? What are your conflicts about?

3. Have you been the culprit attacking people because you are holding on to tradition rather than valuing them?

4. What are the issues that matter to you, which seemingly bother you greatly when in church? Why do those issues matter?

5. What are your values and what are the values of the church? Do they match?

6. Have your values or the church's values changed between the time you joined and now?

7. Have your conversation been draining recently? Why do you think this is the case?

8. Have you been quietly frustrated by conversations with people you thought were close to God? Why?

9. Do you know any "Bible Spitters"? What are their names?

10. Are you a Bible Spitter? How did you become this way? Do you want to change?

11. How do you feel when you someone quotes & relates Bible verses to your personal situation?

12. What are you thinking when someone tells you that you are wrong and uses Bible scriptures to prove their point? Why?

13. Can you recall a time you felt attacked in church because of your views or convictions? What happened?

14. What are 2 ways you wanted to respond? Be Honest.

15. Have you damned anyone to hell? Why?

Chapter 5
Staying Focused

Success is good. We need to celebrate when we achieve but it's not the end. There is always the next goal to accomplish. Therefore, we must remain focused. Let's continue to self-authorize ourselves by writing answers to these questions and taking heed to some of these recommendations. We are BREATHING DEEP now but we must continue to breathe deep **consistently with intent** so these moments can become healthy habits. So stop reading, take a deep breath, and write.

1. When was the last time you threw a party?

2. Pick a date far enough out in advance where the likelihood of someone not coming to the party is minimized.

3. Invite everyone who has invested in you like friends, allies, and people who have heard and not heard about what you've achieved.

4. Allot time to recognize those who directly contributed to your success. People love public kudos.

5. Be Mobile. Let someone else structure the party so you can move around and talk to people. People want to see you. Let someone else have the responsibility of the party. Remember, this is YOUR NIGHT!

6. What are some attacks you've responded positively to? Why?

7. What are some attacks you've responded negatively to? Why?

8. How has these attacks affected your team?

9. How did you manage your team?

10. Have you felt guilty about your accomplishments lately? Why?

11. Is it easy for you to become intoxicated with your success? Why do you think that is?

12. Do you think some of your habits impair your progress? What are some of those habits?

13. Are you a people pleaser? Why do you think that is? Do you think you can change?

Breathe Deep Reprise
Chapter 6
Pressing Onward

Setbacks are difficult places to maneuver. So much is at risk when we have those types of experiences. Yet, there is so much help as well. We've discussed much in this chapter. Take some time to further empower yourself. Answering these questions will give you a greater sense of security in knowing you're not crazy or senile. You are on track and you have what tit takes to endure and succeed. So stop, take a deep breath, overcome your setbacks, and press onward.

1. Think of an event where something went wrong quickly. How did you respond to it? Why?

2. Think of an event where something was personally significant to you and it went horribly wrong. How did you respond to it? Why that response?

3. What names are you calling your setbacks? Are the names you're giving your setbacks invoking positive/negative attitudes? What are the actions proceeding after your naming the setback? Are they productive or destructive? Why?

4. How have you consistently seen your problems? Why?

5. What do your setbacks put you in remembrance of? Why is that situation so vital to how you see life now?

6. Do you remember why you started this journey? What is it?

7. Will you allow life's experiences or people to rob you of your reasons for starting this journey? Why not?

8. Will you use your memory of success over adversity to fuel your drive to finish what you started? Why?

9. Will you finish what you started? Why?

10. Can you still see your dreams after the setback?

11. Will you let people help you? How do you plan to do that?

12. Do you still have faith? How do you know?

13. Are you practicing faith in uncontrollable situations? How so?

14. Do you trust your teammates? How do you know?

15. Do you have more teammates than jersey wearers? How do you plan to keep them or make adjustments?

16. Have you told your teammates you need help or do you expect them to know you need help without your help? Why?

Chapter 7
Intimacy Reality Check

We've spent a considerable amount of time looking at how romantic relationships can throw us off. Let's work through these questions and see if we can avoid some of the pitfalls I've mentioned earlier. Our lives are too precious to hide in pretentious relationships. We need real heat, real intimacy, and real companionship. This may be a little difficult but as I said before, you've made it this far, why stop now? This is our reality check. Let's take our time. Take a deep breath my friend and face the questions of your romance.

1. Have you isolated yourself because of how your setback made you feel? Why?

2. Have you blamed your setback for where you currently are in your life? Why?

3. Have you been looking for romance to substitute your team and validate your escape? Why?

4. How did you initially feel when you reconnected with a past romance? Why?

5. What was your context during the time you met your past romance? How did that affect your interaction with him/her?

6. Was the conversation refreshing? Why or why not?

7. Did you exchange contact information with them? Why?

8. What do you expect to happen between you and your past romance? Why?

9. Has continual phone conversations with your past romance changed your mind over time? If so, how?

10. Have any of your phone conversations started out non-sexual and became sexual? Why did it happen? Did you start out resisting and later on engaged in it? Why?

11. How has talking on the phone with the same person affected your life?

12. What is your personal definition for lovemaking? Why is that your definition?

13. How do you personally define love? From what experiences do you build that definition?

14. Are you afraid to be transparent and vulnerable in your romantic relationships? Why?

15. In your current/previous relationships (where they said they loved you), did you feel they loved all of you or just part of you? Explain.

16. Do you love people for all they are and all they aren't? How so?

17. Have you ever been confused as to whether you just had sex or made love? Why?

18. Have people ever manipulated your romantic desires for their advantage? What happened?

19. Despite your horrible romantic experiences, do you have the courage to believe there are good people who will not hurt you in ways you've already been hurt? Why?

20. Have you been guilty of loving the idea of a person rather

than loving the person? Why?

21. What about the person's present made you not want to acknowledge it?

22. What about the person's future made you want to treat him/her according to it?

23. Why did you choose to stay when it would have been easier to find someone you could be happy with their present?

24. Would you have been in a different mindset to deal with your past flame had you not ran from your problems and abandoned your team? Why?

25. Would your need for romantic intimacy differ had you not separated yourself from the intimacy of your friends and allies? Why?

26. Will your past flame be able to deal with the new you restored, which is significantly different to the old you wounded (the you they met)? Why?

27. Is your past flame adding depth to your new life? How?

28. Is your past flame pursuing a goal compatible with yours? What is it? How is it compatible?

29. What kind of heat is your past flame generating? Is that the kind of heat you need to get you to reach your dreams successfully? Why?

ABOUT THE AUTHOR

Phillip W. Bufford is a speaker, consultant, author, and the CEO of Tip the Scale Consulting, LLC. Mr. Bufford motivates, inspires and empowers his audience to make their lives count for more than a catalogue of memories. Captivating in his delivery and prolific in his approach, Mr. Bufford compels people to seize every opportunity to discover and reclaim purpose for meaningful lives. His passion for people drives his message home in such a way that it makes the message indisputably a message igniting the fire of humanity's soul. His trademark is humor and straight talk. He believes perspective enables us to laugh at life's setbacks. Phillip W. Bufford advocates living life as simply as possible. Convinced that life is difficult by itself, we must do everything we can to keep our approach simple.

Phillip W. Bufford received an Associates Degree in Religious Education, Bachelor of Arts in Religious Studies, and is a candidate for a Masters of Arts Degree in Organizational Management. In addition, Mr. Bufford is a district executive with the Boy Scouts of America in Cleveland, OH and a board member for Cleveland MOTTEP. He is also a proud brother of Phi Beta Sigma Fraternity, Inc. Mr. Bufford has appeared in the *4th edition of Who's Who in Black Cleveland Magazine*, *The Cleveland Plain Dealer*, *The Call & Post*, *The Akron Beacon Journal*, *The Reporter*, and the *Alliance Review* as well has been a guest on 93FM WZAK and 1490AM.

His easy-going personality and friendly demeanor makes Mr. Bufford a well-respected man and a well-loved mentor. His hope-inspiring passion and his dynamic delivery makes him a highly sought after speaker and facilitator.

Phillip W. Bufford is simply – PASSIONATE PURPOSE REBORN!

For more information about Tip The Scale Consulting, LLC go to:

www.tippingthescale.com

ACKNOWLEDGEMENTS

1. Tanya Dixon
   - Thank you so much for everything. You know I blame you for my success (laughing). You know it's your entire FAULT! Seriously though, neither my company nor this book would exist without your continual inspiration, support, and finesse. To say thank you does not do justice for what you truly deserve. Nonetheless, I thank you from the depths of my heart and soul.

2. Mom & Dad
   - Thank you for giving me the foundation to live life with integrity. I'm the reason both of you have grey hairs but thank you for not giving up on me. It's my desire I will be as good of a parent as the both of you have been to Deana, Ericka and myself. We love you both.

3. Kyauna Miller
   - Sweetie, we've been through it all and still stand strong. Thank you for standing by my side. I am not the easiest man to deal with, but you dealt with me nonetheless. There are no words for that kind of commitment. You have encouraged me and taken care of me in ways no one else could ever know about. Thank you. I love you.

4. Deana, BK, and Michael
   - Thank you for being my big sister. You were instrumental in a time when I was broke and practically homeless and you provided me a home to stay in. BK, thank you for making me laugh. Michael, thank you for keeping me company. I love you all.

5. Andre, Ericka, Dre, McKenzie, Eric, Zoë, and the unborn one
    - Hey you guys, all I can say is thank you for giving me the escape of a busy life. Your family has been the source of my hope to have a family of my own. Baby sister, I have much respect for you. Andre, thank you for reminding me there are Black men that don't run from responsibility. And to all the kids, thank you for making me feel like the best uncle in the world. And remember McKenzie and Zoë – no boyfriends until your 105 yrs old.

6. Chester Starks, Jr.
    - We did it playa! All of the emails, conversations, and meetings added up to this. Brotha, what can I say. Yes, I'm talking my Ebonics here. I could not have done any of this without your help either. The brochures, the cards, and the website was all because of your willingness to invest in me and build a network. You have indeed been my business partner, friend, editor, and confidant. You are the man! Thank you for believing in me.
    BLACK IDENTITY!!!

7. Jason Johnson
    - You have been a great and precious friend. When I needed to talk and vent, you were that man. Thank you. You kept me level headed and this is the result. Thank you Big Brother (laughing).

8. Tara Lamont
    - Thank you for pushing me. You kept me busy, girl! You kept my company in front of people and you kept me honest. Moreover, you kept me connected. Thank you for believing in me.

9. Felisa Adams, Gail Thomas, Geno Gates, Sharon Stewart
    - You helped me raise $$$. We've hit over 100% back to back for 2 consecutive years and I could not do it without you all. I can never forget what you've done for the district. You have helped me on committees and more. Thank you.

10. Bishop Romey Coles, Jr.
    Thank you for preaching with integrity. I appreciate your willingness to discuss matters other preachers shy away from. Thank you for being my friend.

11. Elaina
    - Girl, we go back before we had thoughts about losing our virginity. Your friendship is priceless. Thank you for being you.

12. Jamill Taylor-Ashley
    - We've both seen alot. You have kept me thinking about different things as I wrote this book. Thank you for all the emails, phone calls and instant messages.

13. Jacques Smith
    - Thank you for your caliber of leadership with the district. Our outcomes have drastically changed to your support. Thank you for believing in me.

14. Brothers of Phi Beta Sigma Fraternity, Inc.
    - I love you all. Thank you for your brotherhood. You have held me accountable to being what a true Sigma Man is all about. There is nothing more I can say. GOMAB

15. Sisters of Zeta Phi Beta Sorority, Inc.
    - Thank you, thank you, and thank you. You all have

rallied behind me in so many different ways for so many different reasons. All I can say is thank you.

16. Brothers of Alpha Phi Alpha Fraternity, Inc.
    - You brothers are awesome. Thank you for all your support.

17. Vernon "Byrd" Tyus
    - It's official playa. Thank you for believing in me. Let's crank out some stars.

18. T-One
    - Thanks for engineering many of the projects.

19. Deborah Moore
    - You are a true blessing. Thank you for being my 1st client.

20. Collinwood Class of 2008
    - I love every single one of you. Your excitement about life reminds me why I do what I do. Thank you. MAKE YOUR LIFE COUNT!!!

21. McKinley Wiley
    - You are a great friend. Thank you for the photo shoots. Kyauna & I personally thank you.

22. Kevin James
    - Keep pumping out those youth programs. I love our conversations. Cleveland needs you.

23. Delorne Young
    - Thank you for being my little brother. Your faith in me humbles me greatly. Thank you. HEY IESHA!!!

24. Valerie James

- Keep pushing girl. Your commitment reminds me that perseverance doesn't comes easy, but its so worth it. Your Blessing is closer than you think!!!

25. Joe Cook
    - You have helped me with class and been there for our conversations. Thank you.

26. Terry Dziak
    - Thank you for asking all the time about the book. Your inquiries kept me writing. Thank you.

27. Felicia Woods Wallace
    - Thanks for always keeping your door and your school open to me. Thank you so much

28. Rev. Robin Woodberry
    - Thank you for keeping me involved and informed in the NOBDA. I love those kids and it's a pleasure serving them.

29. Charita Crockram
    - Thank you for allowing to inspire the young men at JFK.

30. Keyanna Vaughn
    - I love our conversations. Thank you making me feel like I know what I'm talking about (laughing).

31. John Davis
    - You are an awesome executive. It's a pleasure to work with you and esteem you as my friend.

32. Debra Nash
    - Thank you for the conversations and your faith in me.

33. Jennifer LaRiccia, Tony Diggs
    - It's such a pleasure to provide programming to the youth with you. Thank you for your service to the city of Cleveland.

34. Matt Baker, Chris Moore
    - You boys are some professionals if I've never met any. All I have to say is pop your collars (I know I have to explain that one later – Laughing)

35. Gertrude Wilson, Constance Speed
    - Thank you for your warm smiles and encouraging words. You have no clue how far it goes for me.

36. Edith, Heather, JoAnn, Rose, Shirley, Chris
    - Thank you for all the laughs, covering my back, and keeping me informed. Much of my success is credited to you. I'm still going to keep singing for you ladies (laughing). What's up Edith – Salsa time!

37. To everyone else I've forgotten
    - Thank you for all that you've done. Charge it to my head and not my heart.

38. To all the haters, skeptics, critics, and negative folks
    - Thank you for keeping me focused! Thank you for motivating me to prove you all WRONG!!! Thank you for the resistance! YOU TRULY MADE ME STRONGER! Thank you (laughing hysterically).

39. And last but always first– To My GOD, My Brother, and My Friend
    - Thank you for thinking of me. Thank you for making me. Thank you for dying for me and redeeming me. Thank you for putting up with my foolishness. Thank you for tolerating my ignorance.

Thank you for placing people in my life to guide me. Thank you for forgiving me. Thank you for wiping my tears away. Thank you for showing me your secrets. Thank you for esteeming me worthy enough to have a relationship with you. Thank you for not letting other people kill me when they made plans to. Thank you for not letting me kill myself. Thank you for your grace and your mercy. Thank you for really having a plan for my life. Thank you for every blessing you've given me. Thank you for never abandoning me in the difficult times. Thank you for the people who helped make this book and my company a reality. Thank you for my family. Thank you for Kyauna. Thank you for Tanya. Thank you for giving me hope. Thank you for blessing this book. Thank you for my past, my present and my future. I regret nothing. Thank you for your love. And most of all, I thank you for – YOU! While having your benefits are great – HAVING YOU IS BETTER! THANK YOU!!!